To Rosemary

Thanks for the support
& best wishes!

Anthony L. Baker

Two Wrongs

A NOVEL

Anthony L. Baker

Order this book online at www.trafford.com
or email orders@trafford.com

Most Trafford titles are also available at major online book retailers.

© Copyright 2017 Anthony L. Baker.
All rights reserved. No part of this publication may be reproduced, stored in a retrieval system, or transmitted, in any form or by any means, electronic, mechanical, photocopying, recording, or otherwise, without the written prior permission of the author.

Print information available on the last page.

ISBN: 978-1-4907-8224-9 (sc)
ISBN: 978-1-4907-8225-6 (hc)
ISBN: 978-1-4907-8229-4 (e)

Library of Congress Control Number: 2017906682

Because of the dynamic nature of the Internet, any web addresses or links contained in this book may have changed since publication and may no longer be valid. The views expressed in this work are solely those of the author and do not necessarily reflect the views of the publisher, and the publisher hereby disclaims any responsibility for them.

Any people depicted in stock imagery provided by Thinkstock are models, and such images are being used for illustrative purposes only.
Certain stock imagery © Thinkstock.

Trafford rev. 05/01/2017

 www.trafford.com

North America & international
toll-free: 1 888 232 4444 (USA & Canada)
fax: 812 355 4082

CONTENTS

Chapter 1: Betrayed and Set Up 1
Chapter 2: You're on Death Row, Fool 6
Chapter 3: Windows of the Soul 11
Chapter 4: The Planning Room 16
Chapter 5: Dirty Windows 19
Chapter 6: Big Daddy 23
Chapter 7: Bad Boy 29
Chapter 8: Release the Hounds 36
Chapter 9: Implementation 40
Chapter 10: Brother to Brother 46
Chapter 11: Slavery 52
Chapter 12: Lovely Scenery 57
Chapter 13: D-Day 63
Chapter 14: Don't I Know You? 68
Chapter 15: Reality Show 75
Chapter 16: Unknown Terri-Tory 81
Chapter 17: Sunday's Best 87
Chapter 18: Insert Foot 92
Chapter 19: If You Don't Know Me by Now 96
Chapter 20: Threats and Promises 102
Chapter 21: And the Winner Is 105
Chapter 22: New Shit 111
Chapter 23: Intermission 116
Chapter 24: Wrong Floor 119
Chapter 25: Put into Action 123
Chapter 26: Lunch Date 126
Chapter 27: Want Some More? 129

Chapter 28: Divine Interception 133
Chapter 29: ROI 137
Chapter 30: The Heart Knows 141
Chapter 31: I'm Listening 145
Chapter 32: Let's Get Serious 149
Chapter 33: Meeting Up 151
Chapter 34: What's Love Got to Do with It Anyway? 156
Chapter 35: Proper Paperwork and Product 160
Chapter 36: Wrap Up 164
Chapter 37: *Everything* Is a Choice 167
Chapter 38: Uncovered 171
Chapter 39: Finger Lickin' Good 175
Chapter 40: The Weekend Warriors 183
Chapter 41: Surprise, Surprise, Surprise 188
Chapter 42: The All-Seeing Eye 196
Chapter 43: Loose Ends 199

CHAPTER 1

BETRAYED AND SET UP

Three and a half years. Not a *long* time. Unless you're in prison for a crime you *didn't* commit. This was the fate of one person: Vincent Taylor. Wearing the very same drab black-and-white striped suit the whole time, only having it washed on occasion. He was a handsome guy, smart, well-groomed, six feet two inches, black, and in tiptop shape. He would put you in the mind of a younger version of Maxwell but with a shadow of a beard and moustache. His eyes were kind but serious, and you *knew* when he meant business. He was never the kind that got in any *big* trouble, until now that is . . . just the normal things a kid might find himself doing. But he wasn't a kid anymore, and even though he had done *some* time for menial crimes, it *certainly* was not for murder. However, *that* was just what he was in prison for.

The long corridor that led to the "special room" was nothing more than gray cement blocks decorated with cobwebs and dust along with the smell of fresh piss, musk, and farts. One could see how the mold on the walls had taken residence. Graffiti had to be removed almost on a daily basis. *How* the prisoner got the markers was *always* the unsolvable mystery. Passing by the cells, you could hear sneers, jeers, and cheers for the appointee of the hour. You could *hear* them but could only make out a few phrases. There was no jealousy, however. This was one of those *rare* occasions when being in the cell was a *good* thing for a prisoner. Seeing as how it was February, at the height of the winter season, *and* it was New York, you would have thought *someone* would turn up some heat. But neither the guards *nor* the warden seemed to care. They only cared about getting *paid* and making it alive through the week to collect. A chill overtook Vincent for a second.

The "special room" was nothing more than solitary confinement here at the New York State Prison Facilities. Even though there was nothing *special* about it, the warden got a *kick* out of calling it that, and the guards *quickly* grasped onto the idea. There was no phone, no lights, no motorcar—not a single luxury. Even when the guards would bring the "tray of the day," you could tell that no *well-known* chef put his part into preparing it. This was just *another* so-called fun phrase the guards would use at the expense of the prisoners. It was just enough to sustain a man but just enough to piss him off as well.

Vincent was being escorted down this corridor as the "special guest" of the moment, and for some reason, this walk seemed to go on forever. One could say that this was not a bad thing since he really wasn't in a hurry to *get* to the "special room" anyway. His arms, neck, and legs ached with pain since he had to be subdued by a couple of the guards. Turns out that an inmate had been put up to reaching around Vincent and grabbing him between his legs . . . as a sort of "massage therapy." That particular inmate also thought that if he could get V, as Vincent would be called, to be his pimp daddy in prison, then no one else would mess with him. He figured wrong. V tried to *kill* this inmate but fell short of his task when he was grabbed by who he *thought* was his friend. This inmate would spend quite a few days in the infirmary though.

Officer Kevin Casey was one of those rare guards who too often cared about prisoners, especially about those who were dogged or jumped on by other inmates. He was six feet six inches, weighed 260 pounds, in great shape, and since he was balding on the top of his head, he kept his head shaved. He had a light mustache and goatee, but it was graying in spots. You could see how his job made him *look* a lot older than he was. Even with lotion, you could see how his hands were weathered, and there were a couple of scars on his arms and back from scuffles at the prison that he wore like badges of honor. He was proud to do what he did, so his uniforms were always pristine.

When V first arrived at this prison, a gang of horny inmates jumped him, and Kevin, who just happened to be making his rounds, heard the scuffle. V thought to himself, *Somebody's gonna die before they get this ass! Might be me, but it won't be only me!* Kevin wound up stopping what would have been a painful and embarrassing situation for V, but it also prevented V from killing maybe one or even two of the assailants. Vincent Taylor and Kevin Casey started a friendship from then on, and for three and a half years, V has had his back watched ever since, whenever possible that is . . . except for this last time. V knew Kevin couldn't watch him all the time, so he made sure he would do three things while he was here: He would continue to work out, he would continue the art of jiujitsu that he had practiced since a teen, and he would visit the library as often as he could, if nothing more than to become a little more educated. After the inmates learned that V was convicted for killing a judge and was on death row, it really wasn't necessary to watch his back all the time anyway; he became an instant hero among the *majority* of the inmates. Some couldn't care less, and you know what they say: "You can't please everyone." They knew they had to serve their *own* time for whatever crimes they were convicted for, so hey, "to each his own." And for the ones who were convicted by Judge Mumford, they almost *cherished* V! If Kevin hadn't stopped him, V would have murdered that "massage therapist." Self-defense? Sure, but while in prison, it would have still been looked upon as murder. He was trying to protect his ass *literally*, but because of his actions, he found himself in more trouble and sore as well. He was already accused, convicted, and sentenced for murdering a man *outside* of prison that had no witnesses. But to actually murder someone *inside* of prison that *would* have had *witnesses* would not have been good for V. But the inmates learned another valuable lesson: They knew not to fuck with V.

"Sorry about the chokehold, V. You know I can't just let you *kill* a man in here, no matter *what* he does."

"Just doing your job, huh, Kev?" Everyone else called Kevin "Casey," but a bond was formed between these two men, so "Kev" was acceptable for V. V was pissed, and even though Kevin was a guard, V had come to like him and consider him as a friend, and since he was in his forties, V looked at him like he would an elder brother.

"Come on, man, you *know* I got your back . . . to a degree. You're cool and all, and you know some shit, but a judge is *dead* all because of *your* black ass!"

"Damnit, I *told* you, Kev, I'm *innocent*! Someone framed me, son! I was set up from the get up!" V stopped long enough to look Kevin straight into his eyes. He was obviously upset and in pain, but he was still determined to stand his ground about his innocence. "I didn't do it!"

V's mom always told him that the eyes were the windows to the soul. He just hoped that someone—*anyone*—would look into his eyes and be able to tell he wasn't lying. Kevin *wanted* to believe him, but as an officer of the law, evidence *always* overruled emotions. It had to.

"Man, that's what they *all* say, but you see, I get paid by the hour, not by who I *do* or do *not* believe. If it makes you feel any better, I *want* to believe you."

V, by this time, felt betrayed and hurt by everyone, and seeing that his "friend" didn't believe him, that hurt even more. Sure he was a guard, but in his time on the job, he *had* to have run across a prisoner who was truly innocent of a charge. V could see that talking was getting him nowhere, so he shut up as they reached solitary confinement. Kevin opened up the door to the much smaller and a lot colder cell than the regular ones. It was just a little bigger than an office cubicle, and there was only enough room for one to lie down but not comfortably. There were no sheets or beddings or even a toilet . . . just a hole in the floor to *squat* over. One could tell that no *main* housekeeping was done to this cell. On one wall, there were markings someone put there to keep up with how long they were there. There was a grate in the middle of the floor so when the guards would hose the room off, all the shit, piss, and vomit could just flow down the drain. After that, they would just let it dry out until the next "guest." It *still* smelled of shit, piss, and regurgitations. This time, however, it seemed that they hosed the room right before V got there . . . on purpose. By all means, *no one* wanted to stay here for more than a week.

"See you in a *week*, dude," Kevin said through the cell door's slit. "Yo, V? I'll be checking *in* on you, aw-ight?"

There was no response, but Kevin knew he was doing what he was paid to do, even if it hurt a friend. Kev started to walk away.

"Say, Kev?" V called out.

Kevin turned back to V and got close to the cell. "Yeah, V, what up?"

"Ain't nobody mad. We're cool, man," V said.

Kevin smiled. "It'll be over before you know it," he said. It hurt him to know what V was about to go through, but he knew he had to do his job. He left V to his punishment and his thoughts. A week in solitary was *plenty* of time for a person to think. Good times, bad times, happy times, sad times. At this point, all V could think about was feeling betrayed and how he would get out of this mess. He *was* innocent; he and *God* knew this, but there was *no way* he could prove that while in jail, and God wasn't making any personal appearances on his behalf. His mom got a chance to look in his eyes at the trial, and *she* knew in her heart and soul he didn't do it. She would do what she could for him, and his girlfriend Cassandra *said* she had his back, but V was having his doubts about Kevin. He had a best friend named Junior, but he had no idea where *he* was. And to make matters worse, V had an identical twin brother by the name of *Victor* Taylor. This brother was the <u>best</u> defense attorney in the state and one of the best in the country. Let Victor tell it, he was probably the best in the world. It just didn't make sense that when Vincent was sentenced over three years ago, Victor had not even tried to help his case or even come to visit him. Three years and not even a *phone* call. There was no *card—nothing*. But if the *truth* were to be known, Victor *detested* his look-a-like brother.

That's my brother! My own flesh and blood! How can he just turn his back on me? thought V.

He decided that he'd better think of something else, or he would probably do something he couldn't *fix* or *reverse*. As long as he knew he was innocent, committing suicide was out of the question, so he decided to have positive thoughts about the last time he saw his girlfriend Cassandra. Even *her* visits became less and less, but when she *did* come, wow!

CHAPTER 2

YOU'RE ON DEATH ROW, FOOL

"Hey, Cassie," V said over the phone on the other side of a glass wall.

"Hey, boo." Cassie was looking *especially* good this day. She had her hair braided in those tiny braids that takes eighteen hours to complete. Her Bobbi Brown makeup complimented her dark chocolate skin, not that it wasn't already flawless. She had on some tight-fitting DK jeans, some three-inch black and gold high heels, and a gold silk blouse that looked like it was tailor-made just for her. She carried a black leather coat in her arms and wore a black pin-striped fedora. She was tight, and at five feet five inches, she was the *finest* thing in the neighborhood. At least in *V*'s eyes, she was.

"I miss you *so* much, baby," she said with pouty lips.

"I miss you too, girl. A *lot*! Have you seen or talked to Moms?"

"I see her almost every day. She prays for you *all* the time."

"Okay. What about Vic?" he asked.

"I don't think Victor is praying for you. Hee hee! I'm joking, boy. What about *Victor*? I don't see him that often. I mean, all he does is work at his firm and doesn't at *all* seem concerned with what *you're* going through, but Moms and I are doing all we can to try to come up with *something* . . ." She turned away, and her voice trailed off as if trying to think of the right thing to say.

"Boo? You didn't *really* kill that man, I mean Judge Mumford, *did* you?" Cassie asked.

V exploded. "What the *hell* do you mean, did I kill that judge? You *know* me! I wouldn't kill *anyone*! What the fu . . . You think that I would *kill* a man just because he sentenced me for a few months in juvie years ago? Hell, I'm *over* that shit! I wouldn't kill him for *that*! Hell, I wouldn't *kill* anyone! I *couldn't*! You should know this! *Damn*, girl, I can't believe you just *asked* me that shit!"

V really didn't mean to go off like that, but Cassie hurt him. She was looking so good, but to him, she was talking so stupid. *She doubts me*, he thought. He stared at her like she was a complete stranger. She was supposed to be his girl, his lover, his squeeze; and he didn't want to alienate one of the few people who were *supposed* to be on his side. But right now, the pain of betrayal ruled his emotions.

"I'm sorry, boo. It's just that the evidence is so *strong* against you. I don't *mean* to show you any doubt or act like I don't *believe* you, and I'm *certainly* not trying to upset you. Look, if you *say* you didn't do it, well then, I guess you didn't do it," Cassie said.

V's thoughts were soaring. *You guess? If this is how you really feel, how come you can't look me in the face when you say this? And you still didn't say that you really believe me.*

Everyone's always talking about evidence. Doesn't <u>faith</u> have something to do with evidence too?

"Shit, Cassie. I'm sorry 'bout going off like that. It's just that I need to know you are on my side through all this. It's *obvious* you don't believe me *now*, but I'll tell you what . . . You *better* believe that I didn't do it. It's as simple as that. And there's one *more* thing that you better believe: You *know* that there's *never* been *anything* that I've gotten into trouble for that I couldn't get myself out of. The only difference between then and now is that I didn't *do* anything to *deserve* this. You just wait and watch. A little brainpower and a little time and I'll come up with *something*. You know I'm right, don't you, baby?"

"Damn, V, you're on *death row*, fool! What, you think you're just going to *walk* out the front gates and they're going to just *let* you? You're in deep *shit*, boo!" Cassie said this as if she was trying to *convince* V to accept his fate, not even thinking about how it might make him feel. He just gave her a look that would have knocked her out of the chair she was sitting in as if the reality of being on the opposite side of a glass divider wasn't evident. Cassie tried to atone.

"I'm sorry, babe. You're right. You'll find a way out of this. I *know* you will. And I'm willing to help you any way I can."

At this point, V didn't feel like he could even *trust* her, let alone confide in her anymore. He knew that whatever plan he *might* come up with, it *wouldn't* include her. Not now. In his mind, if you couldn't *believe* him, then how could you *help* him; let alone, why *would* you? Whatever the plan turned out to be, Cassie *definitely* wouldn't be a part of it. He tried to muster up a positive tone toward his lady though.

"Thanks, sweetie. I know you will, and that means a lot. Say, if you see Vic, tell him I'd like to see his sorry ass. Just don't say it like *that*, aw-ight?"

"Sure, boo. I *know* how to talk to Victor. But you *know* he doesn't like *me* either."

"Yeah, I know. If you see him, just *tell* him, okay?"

"Okay, gotcha. Look, love, I gotta run. Love you."

Cassie blew V a kiss as she turned to walk away. Just remembering how she looked from behind was all the motivation he needed to start working out his plan to prove his innocence. Being where he was at the moment, this was *all* he wanted to think about, but more importantly, it was *all* he *needed* to think about. *But how?* V thought, scratching his head.

"Well, well, *well*! What have we *here*? A dog just took a shit right here in the 'special room.' When I found out who the fuck they said was in here, I wanted to bring the 'tray of the day' *myself*!"

Jebediah Cooper was one of those guards who you could smother in their sleep and then have a great night's rest of your own. He was bringing the customary one meal a day for anyone in solitary confinement. Cooper was mean, and he had the kind of face that even a mother would trade in for a baboon. He always looked like he smelled something rotten. It was his fault though. While he was out hunting one day with his father, he stuck his head in an old log, and a skunk pissed in his face. He's looked like that ever since. Cooper had his upbringing in Mississippi, and all he was used to was going to schools with classmates that looked just like him. He really never got a chance to find out what it was like to have a black friend or what the experience would be like to relate to them. His father was the mayor and fought against civil rights in his day. He wanted his son to have the same values as he and taught Cooper hatred and separatism. Cooper made his way North after high school to, as he said, "make a name for himself." He lied on his application and had been working in the penal system ever since he made it to New York. He got married but found out he couldn't have children, which made him even more bitter. This saddened his father, but as long as Jebediah stayed faithful to his teachings of hate, old man Cooper was proud of his son. Had the old man lived to see this year, he would have been ninety-one, but when he died last year of lung cancer, Cooper vowed that he would leave a legacy, if only in name alone. His coworkers used to tell him all the time, "You gotta love yourself." At first, he thought they were paying him homage because of his mean attitude but later found out they were just using an acronym—UGLY—U Gotta Love Yourself. But since he really *was*, he found a way to make the saying a part of who he was. There was one thing that was clearly evident to everyone: He couldn't *stand* V. Judge Mumford and Cooper were fishing and hunting buddies and longtime family friends, traveling to different locations together all over the country but mostly the South. Without a doubt in *Cooper*'s mind, V killed his best friend. There was no way that he was about to just let this *man* spend whatever time he had left before his execution without giving him hell. What makes matters worse, V was a young black man and Cooper headed up a hate group toward *all* minorities.

"Oh, *Viiin . . . slut!* Your *dinner* is here!" Cooper sang out to V. V could hear Cooper hawk up a big wad of snot and then heard the phlegm hit the center of the plate that his food was on. Laughter could be heard by surrounding guards.

"You bastard!" V said. "When I get out of here, you will have a well-kicked ass!" he said, getting angrier by the minute. Cooper thought V meant that when he got of *solitary* was when he would be confronted, and he welcomed the thought of V trying *anything* in prison, but V wasn't talking about solitary; he was talking about *prison* as a *whole*.

"You know what, Vinshit? I'm going to *ask* the warden to release your black ass tomorrow so I can see what the fuck you *think* you're going to do. I hope like *hell* you *do* try something. But hey, if you don't, they still gon' fry your ass *eventually*, and I'm going to be there to witness the whole shebang! But as for now, eat up, you black-ass monkey! There's a lot of *protein* on that plate! Hell, I even brought you a banana!"

Cooper was grinning from ear to ear, but that didn't help matters in the looks department. He shouldn't be so quick to call *anybody* a monkey when he looked like one of those flying monkeys from the *Wizard of Oz*. He knew, however, that he possessed the power, and if V *did* try anything, Cooper and probably half dozen guards would have beaten him beyond recognition. At least that's what everyone would be saying at V's funeral:

"Who in heaven's name is that supposed to be?"
"That don't look like V."
"Aw, boo, they did you bad, baby."
"That is not my son. Lord knows that ain't my Vincent!"
"Good! That's what that no-good bastard deserved!"

CHAPTER 3

WINDOWS OF THE SOUL

While V thought about what one might say at his funeral, Victor Taylor, Vincent's identical twin brother, is the *only* one who could have made that *last* statement. How could he *hate* his brother so badly? They were cut from the same cloth in height, weight, *and* looks. They both grew up to the solid height of six feet two inches; both worked out, so they were cut but not too many muscles. Their haircuts were always the same: low tight fade. It didn't matter if they would get a cut at different times; they were so in tune they would always get the same treatment. One of the main ways you could tell them apart was how they dressed. They were twins, and they grew up dressing just alike . . . that is, until they hit high school. It was then when Victor tried to differentiate between the two. V couldn't afford the clothes that Victor wore, and even when Victor dressed down, he looked like a model out of *GQ*. V was clean too but more of the athletic type. So it did get to a point that unless V decided to dress just like Victor, there was a way to know the difference. Even people would identify them once they could tell the difference by calling Victor *Victor* or *Vic* and they would call Vincent *Vinny* or just plain *V. Another* thing they had in common though, they liked to smell good, so it didn't matter what the cost was; V would have the best . . . just like his brother. Okay, so V didn't always do right by Victor . . . or in life in general. He didn't apply himself in school but always found a way to get by. He didn't become a big-time lawyer like his twin. He even perpetrated Victor a couple of times, which had the police questioning *Victor* instead of V. By the time they found out they had made a mistake, they just dropped the charges to save face. Victor didn't like being hauled in for something his brother did. When they were younger, the switch would be consensual, but as they got older, Victor stopped, and V continued on, and this just pissed Victor off tremendously. It was also motivation for Victor to be on the *right* side of the law and not the wrong side. But the question remained: Was that enough for him to hate his brother? It probably didn't help that V was their mom's favorite either. She *tried* not to show it, but children are not as dumb as we *believe* them to be. They can tell. Moms didn't *love* V more than Victor; she just *liked* him more, if you know what that means. She even thought what V did to Victor was funny, but she dared not laugh out loud or make it known to Victor in the event of hurting his feelings. She knew that even though their looks were identical, their attitudes, mannerisms, and characteristics were *totally* different. Moms knew she couldn't treat them *equally*, but she could at least be fair. They looked *so much alike* that they would trade places just to fool people, and they fooled just about everyone, including their father. This was one of those times when it was okay with Victor. But they couldn't fool Moms. Even when they tried to switch personalities, she could still tell them apart by looking them straight in their eyes. Every. Single. Time. When they were young, she would look in their eyes a lot. She got good at it too. She *had* to. Sometimes a *glimpse* was all that was needed.

"The eyes are the windows of the soul," she told them when they were old enough to understand. "You can tell a lot about a person just by looking in his eyes."

"What about *Dad*? What could you tell about him when you guys were dating?" Victor asked. "Or did you not *look* in Daddy's eyes?"

Victor was very inquisitive about *everything*, and if he wanted to *know* something about anything, he'd just *ask*. In *his* mind, there were no stupid questions, only stupid people for not asking; so he asked them *all the time*. V, on the other hand, learned what he needed to know by observing. He took everything in and applied only what he needed *when* he needed it. He was actually a lot like his father. They stood there in matching overalls, waiting for Moms to answer.

"Your father?" Moms responded. "When Thomas Taylor and I started dating, he only wanted one thing: the *panties*." Moms laughed at saying this, but the puzzled looks that came on the boys' faces were *equally* as funny, which made her laugh even more.

"What did he need with your panties, Mama? Didn't he have his *own* underwear? And what's so *funny*?" inquired Victor. He didn't feel this was wrong to ask. He wanted to know. Moms bit her tongue, trying not to laugh anymore, but when she looked into her sons' faces with that look of innocence and the sincere wanting to know, she burst out laughing even louder than before. She thought that she might better explain this before her little imps received an explanation that wouldn't prove worthy to her boys' intelligence. She also didn't want to hurt anyone's feelings. Victor was already getting agitated.

Moms wiped away tears of laughter. "What I *meant* was your father wanted to have *sex* with me. You *do* know what *sex* is, don't you? Anyway, you boys may not believe this, but I was quite a good-looking girl in high school, if I *must* say so myself."

"You're *still* a good-looking girl, Mama," V chimed in, grinning. This made Moms's grin as well. This was how V used what he learned. Attain cool points *whenever* the opportunity presented itself. Get all you can, can all you get, and then sit on the can.

Thomas and Elaine Taylor had a late start when it came to having children. He was too busy trying to "make a living," so when the twins came, they were both forty-one. It was at this point they decided that for health's sake, they would not have any more and would have to make the best with "just boys." "Moms," as everyone close to her called her, wasn't a fat woman, but she knew she had gained some pounds over the years. She sort of put you in the mind of Mrs. Claus, with touches of gray in her hair, showcasing her wisdom . . . or fatigue. She wasn't flashy or dressy, except for when it was time for church. That's when she would wear the big hats that matched the dresses . . . and the shoes . . . and the *purses*. It's been said that "black don't crack," and even though Moms was obviously getting older, she still looked very good for her age. One thing was for sure about Moms: She didn't mince her words. She said *exactly* what was on her mind.

Moms thought, *To be smart, cute, and a flirt at ten years old! I wonder what life has in store for you, Mr. Vincent Taylor! Or better yet, what do you have in store for this life?*

"Thank you, sweetie," Moms said as she gave V a big hug. Victor stood looking at Moms show his brother affection. He was a little jealous, and a hug would have been nice for him as well, but what he *really* wanted was for Moms to finish her story.

"Mama, did you *finish*?" Victor asked in a huff. Impatience was already part of his attitudinal makeup.

13

"Not quite, but as I was saying, I looked in your father's eyes, which is *very* important when a serious moment is occurring. He told me he loved me *sooo* much and that he *knew* in his heart that I was the one for him. I knew, however, at that *particular* moment, he was just *lusting* for me. I don't doubt he had *feelings* for me, but at *that* moment, he just wanted to lie down with me—you know, like I said before, have *sex* with me. Are you sure you boys know what *sex* is?" Moms asked again.

The boys nodded in unison, even though they didn't. Moms continued.

"Well, I told him I loved him too, but then I said, 'Tommy, if you *really* love me, you won't put any pressure on me to do this now. I've seen too many girls having babies, and the daddies are *nowhere* to be found. I like kissing you, and I like being next to you, and I ain't gonna lie to you and tell you this is easy, but I'm waiting until I get married before going all the way. Can you respect my wishes?' *Well*, you should have seen his face drop and the rise in his pants shrink, but I knew in his mind that if I was worth the wait, then he would honor my wish. I still felt like he got with a couple of other girls in high school, even though I could never prove it. I didn't even try to. I never let him know that I suspected him though."

Moms was a very special person. To even *think* that her husband-to-be slept around on her and she *still* stayed with him is special indeed. Thomas Taylor wasn't the *only* guy in high school, and he wasn't the most popular; he was Moms's choice, and she really *loved* him.

"So if you thought Daddy was with other girls, why did you *marry* him? What if he really *did* get with somebody else?" Victor asked.

"Victor, if you truly love someone, then it matters not what the world says or thinks about you and yours. All that matters is this: if that person loves you and you love them. You've got to accept them with all their flaws, that is, if you choose so. They can judge you if they like, but that is their shortcoming, and they can't put you in heaven nor hell. What they *can* do is *go* to hell for all I care. Oops. I'm sorry about that, boys."

Victor must have been content that the end of the story was just told, so he shrugged and started to walk away.

"Where are you going, Vic? Don't you want a hug from your mama too?" Moms asked with outstretched arms.

"Naw. Maybe later." And with that, Victor went to his room and began reading a dictionary, looking up words he had *heard* that day he didn't know the meaning of.

"I hope I didn't hurt his feelings when I gave you that hug, Vincent. You *do* know that I love *both* of you, don't you?" V nodded.

"I hope *he* knows it too." Moms concern was evident on her face and in the tone of her voice.

"Yeah, Mama, I know. And Vic knows it too. He'll be okay. He's just *spoiled*, that's all." V kissed his mother on the cheek and ran outside to play. Moms was all alone with her thoughts about her sons.

Yeah, Vinny, maybe you're right. But both of you are way too smart for your own britches. Just in different ways.

CHAPTER 4

THE PLANNING ROOM

While thinking about Cassandra and Moms, who just *happened* to be his two favorite girls in the world, V found himself smiling in *spite* of where he was. He thought, *Which one of these two people should I place* most *of my concentration?*

Thoughts about Moms were about how she *always* gave him a positive, good feeling. Thoughts about Cassandra were about how she *always* made him positively *feel good*. V felt a slight rise in his standard prison pants, and that settled it for him. *Cassandra wins! She probably shouldn't though.*

While thinking about what Cassandra had done for him in the past and finding his member getting harder, he realized that he hadn't eaten yet. "Hell, you might as well lie down, son. Ain't nothing happening in here for you," he spoke to his "member." He knew that the tray that was left by Cooper had a "special spit sauce" added to it. He wouldn't even try to eat *around* it. The guards would always leave a slit open in the cell one hour after receiving the "tray of the day" so that the prisoner in this particular cell would have just enough light to be able to see his food. V could see the gleaming snot lying dead center of his plate. Since Cooper didn't spit in the water he brought, V decided that this would be one of those times in his life when he just *wouldn't* eat. He'd had a few before. His family wasn't poor, by no means, but there was that rare occasion when there was more month left at the end of the money. Even a peanut-butter-and-sugar sandwich would have been nice on those occasions, or just a sugar sandwich itself, but neither peanut butter nor sugar was in the house at that time . . . Hell, there wasn't even any bread! V knew the feeling, but now that he was a *grown* man, he could handle it a little better. At least he wouldn't die of thirst, and even though the water was surprisingly cold, *this* would be one of those days. He wouldn't die . . . He'd just be hungry.

"Junior!" V blurted out loud, almost choking on the water. V was so concentrated on his dilemma he had forgotten all *about* this dude. Junior was V's best friend and was someone that knew *all* his best-kept secrets and desires even though they had only known each other since they were both sixteen. This was exactly a year before V's father died. *If Junior was here, he could help me,* V thought. But V didn't even know where Junior *was*. As a matter of fact, he didn't even know what his *own* plan was. Right after high school, Junior would take a road trip *somewhere*. This tradition went on for the past seven years. He would stay away for at least three months, starting right after Christmas, and since this was February, V knew he wouldn't see his friend for at least another month, maybe even two. There were even times that V would ask to tag along, but Junior would always say, "What I do, I must do alone," as if he were rehearsing for a Shakespearean play. V *never* knew where Junior went, even though he tried to follow him once. Junior knew that he was being followed by V, and he took him on such a goose chase V found himself lost in another state. He didn't even realize that the car he *thought* was Junior's was of an old man who drove all the way to the Canadian border. When the man finally stopped to gas up and V pulled up beside him, the old man confessed that he knew V was following him, but he thought he was being followed by his son trying to check up on him. To this day, V *still* doesn't know when Junior made the switch . . . or how the hell he did it. The only *good* thing about Junior's *leaving* was his *returning*. He always had brand new Fubu or Thomas Dean brand clothing and also a pocketful of money, which he *gladly* shared with V. Whatever plan that V would cook up at this moment, he would have to do it *alone*. The only thing he knew for *sure* was that as bad as the relationship between he and Victor had become, he still *had* to see his brother.

"Well, I'll just be damned," Vince whispered. "That's *it*! *That's* the *plan*!" It had finally come to him what he needed to do. It might *not* work, but it was surely all that V had. Victor was a very successful trial defense attorney, and he would at *least* come to see him before his execution date . . . if only to gloat. At least V *hoped* he would. Victor could *surely* help with this plan. He *could*, mind you, but there was no guarantee. The *good* thing was that the date of execution had not yet been set. The *bad* thing was that he didn't know *when* they would set a date of execution. The *ugly* thing was that if an execution date was *before* V could work this plan, then an innocent man would die. V never killed anyone in his life but *still* had to serve time, convicted of murder. There was just too much evidence, just enough to prevent any doubt in a juror's mind that V was guilty. This evidence stood in the way of incarceration and freedom. Seeing as how V had a public defender, raising doubt in the jurors' mind was not a priority of Victor's. He thought V was guilty as well. Number one: The judge that was murdered had already sentenced the defendant in the past on menial crimes with short prison stints. Number two: The murder weapon had the defendant's fingerprints all over it. Number three: the defendant was found in the judge's house at the time of the murder—asleep on the couch. And number four: A file was found that had V's name all in it, implicating him with extortion, bribery, and death threats to the now deceased judge. Now place yourself in the jury; what would *you* think? Well, if you were *Moms*, you would be in *denial*. If you were *Junior*, you would think *set up*. If you were Victor or just about anyone else, you would probably be thinking guilty. But the real questions in V's mind were, *why* would *anyone* want to set him up? And *who* would want to do it? Did his *brother* hate him that much? These were the things that he had to find out, and without a doubt, he *had* to see his brother. Time's a funny thing. It waits for no man; it heals all wounds; it can be well spent, or it can be wasted. You can pass it, or you can kill it; you can run out of it, and it even flies when you are having fun. In solitary confinement, all a prisoner has *is* time; most of it alone, but none of it fun. It goes by real slow too. Depending on how long a person stays in this situation, it could possibly cause a mental breakdown. V had one week. This would be his "productive" time. Time to reflect, to think, to plan. *Hell, time to heal!* V thought while rubbing his sore neck and shoulders.

CHAPTER 5

DIRTY WINDOWS

*D**ing dong!* The doorbell rang at Moms's house. No answer. *Ding dong, ding dong!* The sounds of footsteps were finally heard coming to the door.

"Who *is* it?" Moms called out before even reaching the door.

"It's *me, Cassie.*"

The door opened wide, and Moms greeted Cassandra with a big smile and a hug.

"Hi, Cassandra! How are you doing, hon?" Most people ask that question, not really wanting to know the answer or really even caring. Moms, however, was always sincere.

"I'm doing as fine as I can . . . under the circumstances." Cassandra let out a deep breath as she took off her coat. She looked like the air had been taken out of her sails.

"I *know* what you mean, child. Come on in the kitchen with me. I was just baking some chocolate chip cookies with pecans. You look like you could use a couple, huh?"

"Yes, ma'am, I believe I could probably handle three or four. I knew I smelled something delicious when you opened the door!" They both laughed at her response.

"I like to cook to keep my mind preoccupied. Did you go see Vinny?"

"Yes, ma'am. He *asked* about you."

"I'm not surprised. He's *always* thinking about his mama. You'd think he wouldn't be concerned, seeing as what he's facing. How *is* he? Was he glad to see you? Wait. No need to answer *that*. With what *you* have on, I *know* he was glad to see you!" This brought a smile to Cassie's face. Although she was cute, she looked tired, like she had been staying up way too late. Moms could see it all over her.

"You know, baby, I've been praying for something good to come out of all this. And you know what? I am *convinced* that God will bring it to pass. Just you wait and see. Something good is going to come out of this!"

"I wish I had your positive outlook, Moms. Right now, I can hardly see in front of my face." Cassandra allowed a tear to form and then fall down her cheek. "I think I may have upset your son."

"Who? Victor?" Moms asked. Cassandra popped her head up abruptly and looked at Moms with a surprised look . . . *through* the tears. "You just wait until I see that boy! I'll tell him a few—"

"No, Moms! *Not* Victor. *V!* I told him that since he was on death row, he couldn't think the way he's *always* thought in the *past*. You know *what*? He actually *believes* that he can get out of any situation, even *this* one. That may have been true in the past, but *now* . . ." She let her sentence trail off into silence as she turned to look at the window.

"Cassandra, *look* at me." Moms grabbed her hands, looked her dead in her eyes, and tried to reassure her. "I want you to remember something: It ain't *over* 'til it's *over*. And it ain't over *yet*. You just have to *believe*, child. That's all there *is* to it."

"Okay, if you *say* so." Cassandra wiped her eyes and then changed the subject. "Have you *heard* from Victor?" she asked.

"He just left here about twenty minutes before you got here. He said he had to take a business trip and that he'd be back in about a week. He said it had *something* to do with some big trial that was coming up. That *Victor*! Big-time lawyer. I'm so *proud* of my boys! Why do you ask?"

"Well, V wanted me to ask Victor to come see him, even though I know he probably won't. But I'm *curious* though. I can *see* you being proud of Victor. He's *learned*, he's a successful *attorney*, he's *well-groomed*, and he's *rich*. *I* can see that. But how can you be proud of V? *Why*? He's in *jail*! For *murder even*! Moms, you know that this ain't the *first* time that V has been in jail! I just don't *get* it. I mean, I'd like to believe he's innocent too but . . ." Cassandra seemed like she had been let down by V, but at this point, she was raising her voice and didn't even realize it.

"*First* of all, Ms. Cassandra, don't you *ever* raise your voice to me again! I don't allow it from my sons, and I *ain't* gonna allow you or anyone *else* to do it. I just won't *tolerate* disrespect. Hell, even my *husband*, Thomas Taylor, didn't raise his *voice* to me. God rest his soul. He raised his hands a couple of times, but he wound up with a black eye once and a stabbed hand another time. Disrespect me? *No one* is going to do it, especially in my own home. And second of all, if you don't know my Vinny by now, then he may as well be a stranger to you. It's not *where* you are or *what* you have that defines you as a person. It's your *character*, baby, the way you *carry* yourself, the way you treat *others*. It's a lot more inward than outward, and *trust* me when I tell you . . . God is watching and taking notes. Man is *always* looking at a man's outward appearance, but God looks at the heart!" Moms turned and looked out the kitchen window and noticed a squirrel playing in the backyard. Thoughts of how her husband turned out to be for the boys before his death had tears trickling down Moms's face. She turned back around to face Cassandra, wiping away her tears.

"A person is a lot like a book, and you can't tell what the story is about until you read what's inside the book, not the outside cover. And you certainly can't tell the end of a story until you read all the way *until* the end of a story. Then, and only then, can you determine if the story is good or if it's bad. I can *clearly* see some of Thomas in my Vincent, and I like what Thomas tried to instill in him. Sure Victor applied himself a little more, but Vinny's going to turn out to be a fine man. Thomas did, and so will Vincent. Do you *hear* me?" Moms's eyes were still teary but determined.

"Yes, ma'am, I *hear* you." Cassandra paused. "I apologize for raising my voice . . . I'm sorry. But I do have one more question for you, *if* I can ask. I don't mean to upset you, and I surely don't mean to disrespect you, but if V *is* executed, *then* what, Moms? How can V turn out to be anything but *dead* at that point? Where is the *positive*?" Cassandra just *knew* she had made the final and most important point in the conversation. It seemed that her goal in life was to make everyone else accept *her* truth.

"Hon, if Vincent *is* executed, even if it's not for his *own* good, it will be for *someone*'s good. The Bible says that *all* things work together for the good of them that love God, and *all* means <u>all</u>. And I know what you're thinking—Vinny may not love God the way he should, but I do, so it has to apply to me. Here, girl, *have* another cookie."

"Thanks, Moms," Cassandra said while grabbing two. She looked at her watch. "Well, I gotta go, but I'll probably check in on you in a couple of days, okay?"

"Child, go on and do what you have to do. And you don't have to check on me *every* day or every *other* day. I'm fine, child, just *fine*. If I need you, I can *call* you. Right?"

"Okay, Moms, you're right. You better lock up behind me. Oh, can I ask you one *more* question?"

"*Anything*, baby. What *is* it?"

"Can I have some more cookies? These are *good*! Ha!"

"No, you'll ruin your figure," Moms said. Cassie stood there looking surprised.

"I'm just *kidding*, girl!" Moms laughed. "Here you go." She handed her the plate, and Cassie grabbed about three more cookies and headed out the door.

"Love you, Moms."

"Love you too, hon. I'll see you."

Moms locked the door and then headed back to the kitchen to finish her baking. She started humming a tune that could have been Thomas's and her love song or either one of them. Whatever the case, right in the middle of her humming, she stopped and thought to herself about Cassandra's eyes. *The windows of that girl's eyes needed some Windex.* Something told Moms that Cassandra's motives were not quite right. It was all right there in the eyes.

"Damn near ate up *all* my cookies too!"

CHAPTER 6

BIG DADDY

Thomas Taylor, the twins' father, had not always been the best father or husband, for that matter, that he could be . . . not at first. He tried but never could get it quite right . . . not at first. Thomas used to gamble, and when it seemed like he couldn't win, he drank . . . at first. He laid his hands on Moms only those two times she mentioned, but the boys . . . well, let's just say they got it when *he* felt they needed it. He didn't abuse them, but he whipped the *hell* out of them when warranted, which happened to be a lot. He was very careful not to touch *anyone* after he had had a few . . . uh . . . too many nips. But the condition he stayed in kept him in and out of jobs.

One night he gave his family quite a scare when he came home all bloodied and beat up by a couple of guys he owed money to. They wound up taking the watch the boys had given him for Christmas and his *last* $30. Victor was so upset about the watch being stolen and how much they had paid for it that he didn't talk to his father for a week, but V was concerned on whether his father would be okay. Thomas still owed the guys $2,300, and they said they would give him a couple of weeks to come up with the rest. If he couldn't pay, then they would probably break a finger or two or maybe even something more. They just thought that a lesson should be taught to let him, and *others* that owed them know they were not going to tolerate late payments. *Somebody* had to be their "punished" example. After that day, they made a name for themselves that *everyone* in the neighborhood would call them, the Punishers.

But Thomas made a name for himself as well, or as he liked to call himself, Big Daddy Thomas Taylor. These two men should *never* have let two weeks pass by because Thomas befriended a man from New Jersey by the name of Antony Sabino. How they met, no one really knows, but Sabino turned out to be a lifesaver for Thomas. Thomas had a sense of humor that Sabino appreciated, and Thomas Taylor could always make the man laugh. Guess that was enough. He placed Thomas, or Big Daddy, in a big-time position in his personal "operation," and before long, the Punishers were answering to *Big Daddy*. Of course, the $2,300 note was squashed. Thomas stopped drinking; not completely, but not so much that he would make stupid decisions; and after making and saving a substantial amount of money, about $475,000 in a span of two years, he decided that he wanted *out* of this type of business. Someone might say that $400,000 ain't a whole lot of money to live off of, but Thomas had everything paid off, wasn't making any big expenditures, and didn't plan on blowing it on frivolous items.

Sabino hated to see his most trusted and successful "employee" leave, but he cut a deal with Big Daddy, where he would walk away from his "accounts receivable manager" position and become plain old Thomas Taylor, husband and father. This included a retirement package, rewarding him for his loyal and thorough service. Moms was sure glad to hear that Thomas wanted out. It wasn't all about the money with her. Sure she would experience some nice amenities and her house was paid for, but she was always afraid for Thomas's life, seeing as how she *really* didn't know what he was into. She had her suspicions but no proof. His life was more important to Moms than any amount of money or material things.

The boys had gotten accustomed to a different lifestyle that they found to be enjoyable, so for their father to walk away from what seemed to be probably the easiest and highest-paying job that he would ever have just didn't make any sense. They didn't really know what he did and didn't consider the dangers that might have come with the job and, obviously, didn't care. They just loved the attention, power, and money they had at their disposal. How many other twelve-year-olds can brag on having hundreds of dollars in their pockets and not worrying about anyone taking it from them? Even after learning how dangerous it could have been, Victor *never* forgave his father for it. As long as Daddy was popping off a $300 a week allowance, Victor was happy. When the allowance dropped to $20 a week, so did Victor's respect for his father. V couldn't understand why he left either, but at least he forgave him and respected his decision.

Thomas went back to blue-collar work. "That," he said, "is where I feel more comfortable . . . and safe." There just happened to be a new warehouse foreman opening on the outskirts of the city, so Thomas applied for it. He was hired on the spot. He should have been leery of that, seeing as how he hadn't worked anywhere in two years. Not a *real* job anyway. Someone was behind him getting this job so quickly, and it was Sabino. Even when he thought he was *not* working for Sabino, he was back on Sabino's payroll. Sabino just *genuinely* liked Big Daddy, and he wanted to help him out any way he could. Thomas tried to do the right thing, and he was a proud man, so if he had *known* that Sabino was behind his hiring, he would have quit right then and there. He thought he was "the man" and that his *own* credentials were *surely* all that was needed to lock down that position. And for the next five years, he really *was* the man. But as fate would have it, before going home from work, he decided he'd treat his crew to a few rounds of beer. Not to get drunk, just to celebrate a great week of productivity. Someone suggested a bar located even farther out from where the warehouse was, but hey, as far as Thomas thought, life was good, and his employees were worth it. Sabino even showed up, seeing as how someone tipped him on to the celebration. Thomas never thought anything about it. He was glad to see him though. They had a good time, shooting pool, shooting the shit, and shooting down some drinks . . . some taking a few too *many* shots.

One attendee, in particular, was too drunk to drive, and since this was Thomas's idea, he volunteered to drive the guy home. Sabino even offered to ride along. The man was plastered and could hardly tell how to get to his house, but Thomas finally got an address, and he headed toward the destination with passengers in tow. They had to drive down what looked like an old country road, and Thomas began to wonder if he would find his way back to his *own* house. He got the guy safely inside his place of residence and then headed back down that old road. It was late, and he was sure that Moms was worrying a little by now. That's when it hit him—he had done too much drinking and just wasn't thinking. He had his cell phone with him but never even *thought* to call her and tell her what his plans were. She wouldn't call him because she felt like it was checking up on him, and she didn't feel like she should or even had to. She treated him that way the entire time she knew him. He was a man and was taking care of business. *You big dummy*, he thought to himself. Just as he finished punching in the numbers to his home phone, he looked to the left and noticed a family of deer, about five of them. All of a sudden, they darted out in front of his car, using the headlights to light their way. The car swerved just in time to miss two fawns, a doe, and a small buck. But there was a larger buck with them, some might say a twelve-pointer. Thomas didn't miss him. As this deer leaped to try to clear the car, his back legs were caught by the front bumper, which redirected the deer's antlers toward the windshield. The brakes were slammed on but not in time, and in fact, they locked up. Thomas found himself with the antlers of a large deer penetrating the windshield of his car, and to make matters worse, they were headed for a large pine tree. If a car crashes into a tree in the forest and no one is around, does it still make a sound? The answer to that riddle may never be answered, although there was the sound of a small explosion that filled that area. Shards of glass permeated the air like a constellation. The massive head of this buck crashed completely through the windshield of the car after impact and the passengers' faces, heads, upper bodies, and even throats were sliced by this beast's rack. The twisted metal of the 2006 SLK350 Mercedes-Benz Brabus intertwined with the tree and broken legs of this ungulate, creating an abstract art piece that only Picasso would appreciate. The smell of gas and blood-soaked raw meat mingled together, forming a nauseating and unstable scent. Even though the airbags deployed, it was still not enough to impede the cohesion of animal antlers and human flesh. By this time, Moms had answered the phone and could hear all kinds of commotion. Glass and the windshield frame being reshaped as the animal struggled to free itself, excessive anguish brimming over with intense pain, the expelling of a last and desperate breath . . . animal and human. Silence. Dropped call. Moms's worst fears loomed over as she sat staring at the phone in her hand. She called back but no answer.

The funeral director, who was a close friend to the family, told Moms that what she *really* needed to do was to remember Thomas the way he *was*, and he suggested two things for her. Since *he* said that he knew it was Thomas, the first thing he suggested was that she *not* view the body before, during, or after the funeral. It would be too much for her and the family to take in and deal with mentally for the rest of their lives. The second thing he suggested was that she should have a closed-casket funeral. Moms trusted the director but still asked him to prove to her that it was Thomas that died in that accident. He was adamant that she not look at his face and neck and told her that it was way too gruesome and he didn't want her to have nightmares about her husband for the rest of her life. Moms said that she understood, but he would still have to produce some proof, something, so that she could truly believe it was Thomas and not someone else. He had her come to the funeral home and took her to the back where they prepare the bodies. As they walked down the halls, passing the different rooms and the chapel, she could detect the perfume of embalming fluid and alcohol. He took her over to a big burly body covered from head to toe with a sheet. He lifted the bottom of the sheet and showed the feet.

"Okay. The feet of a black man. So what? I don't remember what his feet looked like. Is this my Thomas, or ain't it?" she asked.

He then took her to the side and lifted the sheet to reveal an arm.

"And?" she asked, not really wanting the full answer to this one-worded question.

He turned to the inside of his arm and showed her a tattoo that read, **"T & E! Thomas & Elaine! Totally & Eternally!"** Moms dropped her head, shed a tear, and then returned to her vehicle.

The funeral was held the following Saturday to give enough time for his family that may have been out of town to make the funeral. They made sure that a huge photo of Thomas was placed beside the casket so that people could see and remember him in an unharmed state. The last time Moms saw her husband alive was the morning of his big celebration with his employees. He had kissed her on the forehead while she was still in bed. She was glad she was not asleep when he kissed her, so now she can rely on this memory to be a fond one. Other family members that had traveled far and abroad to be there wanted the casket to be opened, but Moms trusted the funeral director and stuck to her guns.

"That was a very nice service, Ms. Taylor," a young man said to Moms as they walked away from the burial site.

"Thank you, sweetie. I already miss him so."

"I can *imagine*. He was a good man from *my* experience with him. Why was everything so closed off?"

"The funeral director felt it would be best for everyone. He said that Thomas was messed up pretty bad. No one needed to see him. Not even me. We all just need to remember him."

"Oh. I don't know if I would trust anyone *that* much. I would have to see the face for *myself*."

"Well, young man, you'll learn that you have to trust *someone* in this life. The director has been a longtime friend of our family, and I can't see why he would steer me wrong. Besides, he proved it was him."

"Yeah, I understand that. I guess if that was my dad or husband or wife or good friend, even if the accident left them unrecognizable, I just feel like I'd owe it to myself to see him. Ms. Taylor, I'm sorry if this is upsetting you."

"Not at all. I appreciate talking to you younger folks. I hope I can impart some wisdom and at the same time pick up on some things I didn't know."

"Oh okay. So did you learn anything from me?" The young man cocked his head to the side, waiting for an answer that would validate what he has gained in his short life.

"Sure did . . . You're a *busybody*. You'd do well to mind your *own* business in life."

The young man stopped walking and had a disappointed and surprised look on his face.

"You're *kidding*, right?"

Moms laughed. The young man started to laugh a little as well. She turned to face him.

"No, sir, I'm *serious*. You need to learn how to stay in your own lane and let others stay in theirs. Just because it's good to you don't mean it's good to everybody. Understand?"

The young man's laughter stopped, and his smile left his face. He caught up to Moms.

"Yes, ma'am," he said while dropping his head. He had nothing more to say as he walked Moms to the limousine. All Moms could do was smile.

CHAPTER 7

BAD BOY

Prestige. Respect. Wealth. *These* were what Victor wanted ever since his father "walked away from the money." Victor L. Taylor, Attorney-at-Law. Seeing that phrase on all his stationery, letterhead, and even *building* was what he lived for. "Show me the money" was the phrase he liked hearing the most though. The phat rides. The expensive clothes. The big house. The fine wife. The traveling. The parties and events. The unlimited access to women . . . on the side. Yes, *this* was the life for him. And *winning*? He liked winning more than *all* these things, but *having* all these things, in *his* mind, *made* him a winner. Winning a court case was like the most potent drug on the market, and it gave him an internal high, especially if he *knew* his client was guilty. He *was* good at what he did. Actually, he was a *great* lawyer. His nickname should have been Midas because everything he touched seemed to turn to gold. When he was in high school, he had the highest grade point average in the history of the high school being built: 4.45. Now how do you make over four-point *anything* on a four-point-grade scale? To say that he was smart was like saying the Hamburglar *liked* hamburgers or that the Frito Bandito had to have a *couple* of corn chips. The brother was *sharp*. He even graduated a full year before he should have. This pleased him because he would finally be at a place in his life where he and his brother would have to compete being a Taylor twin. He made a score of 120 on the law school admission exam with the highest score *supposedly* to be 100. Went to Columbia Law School and graduated at the top of his class. Passed the bar exam with flying colors. He met his wife Terri while in law school and married her a year after he graduated at the age of twenty. She was two years older, but he carried himself with such maturity she overlooked his age. She looked like a model, so she would do for his image. Did he love her? Even he couldn't answer that question honestly. "She'll do," he would tell himself. He started his own firm one year later and recorded one of the highest most wins to losses ratio in law history, with more wins than losses. Over the years of having such a successful legal career, he would punish any associate from his office that lost a case by giving them research assignments for other cases he had to defend. This, however, was a rare occasion. In Victor's mind, being a defense attorney was the only attorney to be. To stand in front of twelve men and women persuading them to give the verdict for his client that he desired, even if he thought his client was guilty, was like having sex with more than one woman. He had done *this* on more than one occasion as well *while* he was married, no less. He was careful but destructive all at the same time. He was on top of the world, at least in his mind. When he and his brother Vincent were younger, Moms would try to teach them morals that would help them handle life's situations. Victor would always look at it as meddling. He felt—no, he *knew*—that he would control every situation he would be involved in. And he felt, with enough money, there was nothing or no one that could not be bought. *Every* man had his price.

"Pride comes right before a great fall, Victor," Moms was telling Victor. He had just brought her over to his house and was bragging about his ten-thousand-square-foot mansion. It was her first visit.

"But, Moms, have you ever seen a master bedroom this big? And what about that kitchen downstairs? Hmm? I'll bet you could burn some groceries in there, couldn't you? I mean, come on, Moms, you can't say that you're not *proud* of your son."

"*Of course*, I'm proud of you, but you need to carry yourself with some humility and character. Sure you've worked hard for the things you have, and you probably deserve all this. But, Victor, you may not *always* be in the position you're in, and just in case you *do* fall, you need to be prepared when you return back to earth."

"I've been trying to tell him that *myself*, Moms." Terri had just gotten back from playing some tennis with his secretary.

This mansion, as *some* would call it, was supposed to be a present to Terri. Victor thought it would be enough to appease her when she didn't get any emotional support or physical attention from him. The house was laid though. The house was fenced and gated, and the estate could only be entered if you knew the code or code phrase. The long winding driveway that led to the house reminded you of a long road that would lead to a secluded hotel or cottage. But this was no cottage. *This* was a *house*. A mini mansion or, to some, a *mansion* itself. Someone might describe it as a *big-ass* house. Four-car garage with about fifteen steps leading up to the front door, brick and white cedar. When you enter the house, the first thing you see is a huge stairway that leads to the upstairs. To the left of that was a hallway that led to two separate full bathrooms that adjoined with their own bedrooms. These had to be guest bedrooms, seeing how Victor and Terri lived alone with no children. As one would pass the bedrooms, a long hallway would lead to the kitchen, with its many cabinets and granite countertop island with built-in grill and sink. Extra sinks were on the wall with a detailed monochromatic backsplash. The house flowed with an open floor plan that also showed off the den from the kitchen, where Victor would entertain guests. To the right of the den was the study, where Victor had a marble desk, big leather chair, and books all around the walls. He read a lot because he had heard that "readers are leaders." Not far from the study was a door that led to the garage. Around the corner from there was also a little something that Victor *required* for him to feel successful: an indoor heated swimming pool. Upstairs harbored a huge master bedroom with lots of sitting area and walk-in closets for both Terri *and* Victor. The bed itself was probably bigger than any king-sized bed should be. Ever hear of a *pope-size bed?* Didn't think so. The lavatory consisted of a humongous shower with jet heads from every angle, a steam room, a water closet with a TV installed, a double vanity with lots of storage space, and a jetted *three*-person hot tub . . . just in case.

"Shut *up*, Terri! Just *shut* the hell *up!*" Victor responded to his wife. He hated to be scolded by his mother, but when his wife agreed with her, it made him *livid*. At that moment, he felt like he was being double-teamed and belittled, and he was not about to have that.

"Don't get mad because someone *other* than me is trying to talk some sense into you. We're only *concerned* about you and don't want to see you get *hurt*," Terri said, trying to sound reassuring, but clearly, she was fussing. She went over to Moms and kissed her on the cheek. Inside, Victor was pouting like a little boy, but he tried real hard not to show it.

"How long have you known me? Haven't I always been on top? *Trust* me, Terri, and you *too*, Moms, I'm *always* going to be on top! I have insurance you know nothing of, so stop *sweating* me! By the *way*," Victor said while looking at his watch and then his mother, "if you can't support *me* in the things that I *do* or the things that I *have*, then *maybe* you shouldn't come over here anymore!"

That hurt Moms as much as being stabbed with a *spoon*. She never thought that either of her sons would choose material objects over her or disrespect her so.

"Victor, *what* the *hell*...?" Terri blurted.

"No, no, Terri, that's okay. If my son does not want me to be at his home, then this is my first and *last* visit here. Maybe. Nice home, son. I've never wanted anything but the best for my boys, but I thought I had at least instilled some common sense in you two. Well, at least one of you..."

"At least one of us, *what*? You're trying to say that *V* has common sense and I *don't*? His black ass has been in trouble with the law on *more* than one occasion! In prison *now*! You're talking that crazy shit! You know what? Grab your coat. I love you, Moms, but you have to leave. *Now! Terri* will take you home."

With that said, Victor walked out of the room in a huff and went to his study. He locked the door behind him because he didn't want his mother or his wife to walk in on him and see him break down. The teardrops were coming. He had feelings, but he also had an image to uphold. He couldn't look weak to *anyone*, especially not to the ones who were closest to him. He *always* had to win and to exude confidence and control *even* at the expense of hurting others. He needed *that* just to breathe.

* * *

Terri had some of the prettiest brown eyes you would ever want to see, but as Victor walked out of the room, she used those same beautiful brown eyes to give him a look that was as cold as a polar bear's pee hole. Terri had model-like features with brick house measurements of 36-24-36. She was five feet seven inches with legs that went all the way up. As a matter of fact, it was her legs that got Victor's attention in the first place. She was always wearing a skirt or shorts that would highlight her greatest assets when she sat down and crossed them. At that time, Victor knew how to be the perfect gentleman. He would look her straight in her eyes, open doors, whisper sweet nothings in her ear, and hope like hell she hadn't heard about the "windows of the soul" philosophy that Moms always talked about. After they were married, though, things changed abruptly, especially after work at his firm took off. It was at *that* point Victor felt he just needed to be successful in his career to be happy, and that, in turn, would make everyone in his life happy as well. What's love got to do with it, right? Money cures *all* ails, right? At one time he believed that a child would make him happy but squashed the thought when it occurred to him how much *more* responsibility would be added to his already busy life. He didn't need any more responsibility; he needed and wanted more money and prestige. He would do whatever it took to *make sure* that Terri did *not get pregnant*. If she did, he even thought that he *might* not claim the child, which is a coldhearted accusatory denial. If he had *anything* to do with it, there would be *no* kids now, maybe not *ever*.

Terri hugged Moms and handed her some Kleenex to wipe away the tears Moms just couldn't contain any longer. She knew in her heart she had done the best she could with her sons, and that was *all* she could do. They weren't her babies anymore. They were grown men now, and they had to make their own lives, dealing with what life threw their way. Both Moms and Terri sat down on the bed.

"I'm sorry about that, Moms. Vic thinks he has *all* the answers. He's good—*real* good—at what he does as a matter of fact. And yes, as you can see, we have some nice things. I just wish he didn't throw them in everyone's *face* all the time."

"I know what you mean, baby. What about me getting some *grandchildren?*"

"Forget about it, Moms. He's not interested."

"*Really?* Oh . . . really? Well. I guess, right now, I need to be more concerned about his relationship with Vincent. Do you know if they've been in contact with each other?"

Terri cringed at the answer she was about to give Moms. She didn't want to hurt Moms any more than she already was *or* worry her.

"Well . . ." Terri paused, trying not to look in Moms's eyes.

"What is it, Terri?" Moms *was* worried now.

Never pause when answering a question. A pause will throw someone off or draw them in. Be direct and precise. *Never* pause. Terri had learned *that* in law school, so now that she *did* pause, she either had to make up a story or tell the truth. She wouldn't feel good about her answer anyway, and since making up a story would require too much thinking at this point, Terri decided to tell the truth.

"Well, a few years ago, Victor and I went downtown to look at an apartment he was thinking about acquiring. He said he wanted a *woman's* perspective. It was nice enough . . . I would stay there if I were single. Anyway, it was a pretty cold day, and on the way back, we saw Vincent walking. This was before he got put in jail. I asked Vic if he would pick him up, but he didn't say a word. He kept driving right past him. He never even looked his way. About a mile down the road after passing him, Vic just said, '*Hell*, no!' Since V has gone to jail, Victor hasn't even *mentioned* V's name—that is, until today. I'm sorry, Moms."

Moms made sure to look in Terri's eyes when she said this and knew right away that she did not lie, and as Terri suspected, it saddened Moms to hear it.

"My boys. Even though they switched places with each other, not all the times with the other's consent, Victor just can't seem to forgive his brother for portraying him, and now that he's a successful lawyer and Vinny's in trouble, I guess this is Victor's way of paying him back. I've told them many times that two wrongs do *not* make a right."

Moms looked down at floor as if she might have noticed a bug or a spot. For some reason, Moms didn't want Terri to look at *her* in the eye. Terri searched Moms's face, trying to make eye contact just to let Moms know she was there for her.

"But," Moms continued, "three rights make a *left*!" Moms laughed so hard that Terri couldn't help but laugh with her. Moms wasn't trying to hide an expression; rather, she was setting up for the punch line for one of her corny jokes, using the pause on purpose that draws one in. It just gave her a reason to allow her tears to come without pain.

Victor came back into the room.

"Are *you* still here? And what's so *damn* funny?" he asked.

Terri had had enough.

"You *asshole*! *Stop* being mean to your mother! Sorry for the language, Moms."

"No, baby. You don't have to apologize to me for my son disrespecting me. And you know what? You're right. He *is* acting like an asshole at the *moment* anyway." Moms gave him a disappointed look but then surprised him.

"Victor, God *loves* you, and I love you too. But since I am no longer welcome in your home and you *seem* to be upset with me, are you and your lovely wife coming over to *my* house for dinner this coming Sunday? I just happen to be fixing all your favorites."

Victor didn't have to think real long and hard about what his answer would be.

"Even banana pudding?" he asked, looking away. He already knew what the answer was.

"Why, of *course*, silly!"

"Well . . . I *guess* so . . . if you really *want* us to." He couldn't even look at Moms because of the emoted position he was in.

"Yes, I *want* you to. I *insist*, if that *means* anything. So I *expect* to see you two there. Terri, you can take me home now. I would ask Victor to change his mind and take me, but hey, my son is *so* busy. Right, Victor? Anyway, bye, baby. I will see you Sunday." Moms kissed Victor on the chin.

As Moms was leaving, Victor was thinking about the small victory that he felt like he just received. *I'm a bad motherfucker! I just threw my mother out, and she's still fixing me banana pudding!*

CHAPTER 8

RELEASE THE HOUNDS

The past is always something you can do a lot of reflecting on. You *should* be able to learn a lesson from the experiences and mistakes you make in life. V had an entire week to think about his life. The "special room" had been a blessing to him in a way. He had the necessary time to make some important decisions and plans without any distractions. For one, he decided that once he got out of prison, he would make sure not to do *anything* that would get him placed there again. But then he had to remind himself that he didn't do anything to get himself placed in prison *this* time anyway. So he conceded that God would be the only one that controlled that decision. Maybe V needed to give *him* more time. Two, he had decided to ask Cassandra to be his wife. He really wasn't sure what her answer would be, but he knew she would be good for him and he would be good *to* her. Three, he had all the time needed to come up with the perfect plan to find out who framed him and why they did it. He *had* to clear his name. His time in solitary confinement was up, and he knew he had to watch his p's and q's if his plan were to work. No matter what anyone did to him, he couldn't do *anything* to jeopardize his chances to talk with his brother. No back talk. No retaliations. No problems. It wouldn't be long now before the guards would escort him back to his cell with Big Percy. V was just glad that he still had the capacity to think clearly. If only his ace Junior could be here to help pop this off. *Well, I guess I'll have to brag about how I pulled this off by myself next time I see him.* Junior wouldn't believe it at first, but V knew that Junior would support and help him 110 percent. That was one worry V did not have. That is, if he were here. He also wondered what Cassie was doing with herself while he was locked up. She couldn't see him for an entire week, and he started to think not so much as to *what* or *how* she was doing but rather *who* might be doing *her*. This wasn't the best of thoughts, but it became more and more difficult to think that she *wasn't* seeing someone else. *She is faithful, though, isn't she?* he thought. Oh well, pain was nothing new to V, but it didn't mean he had to like it. He just hoped she was still waiting for him to come up with a plan or at least waiting for him—period.

When he was seventeen, and right before his father died in that freak deer accident, V was just beginning to turn his life around. One A, two Bs, and three Cs. He was about to graduate with a grade point average of 2.66. Nothing like his studious brother, but not bad for a guy who hadn't even tried before. When his dad died, he didn't lose his grades; he lost his motivation. As far as he was concerned, he had lost a very important person and a necessary component in his life. He had lost his best role model. Instead of dedicating his life to be even better than his father, he rebelled against life and decided to take what he could have easily paid for. *Besides,* he would think, *it isn't a crime if you don't get caught.* He wasn't a bad kid, he just needed a little more direction before becoming a man, and there was one thing he learned: Age does not always make you a man. Responsibility, character, honor, respect for others—*these* are some qualities that make someone a man. The pain of losing his father was almost unbearable and he felt like life owed him something that it really could never pay, most of all, a chance for his father to see what kind of a man V would turn out to be, who he would marry, what kind of career he would have, where he would live, what the grandchildren would look like if V would ever have any children. He felt cheated and betrayed by life. It owed him his father but couldn't deliver. "Damn it!" he cried out. The guard passing by mistook this outcry as V showing expressions of regret for his in-prison actions.

"Maybe, next time, you'll think before you act, dumbass."

V wiped his tears with the sleeve of his shirt but didn't respond. This guy didn't know what V was going through. But the thoughts about what he would do as soon as he got out of this hole ran over and over in his mind.

"Say," V called out, "how much longer am I in here for?" He was getting anxious and was ready to make his move. He had counted the days, and he knew it wasn't that much longer.

"You got about ten more minutes, unless you fuck up while you're in there. Someone will come get you in a few. Can you wait ten minutes, or should I call the president?"

"Do you have his number, or do I have a choice?"

"Hell naw! Dumbaoo!"

Don't respond anymore, man. That's just what they want, V thought. *A reason.* He knew that for the rest of his stay, they would try *anything* to make him lose his cool. One thing was for sure: He needed to see his brother. His brother was the no. 1 attorney in all of New York. He never lost a case he *personally* worked on as if by magic or something. He had influence and pull on judges, congressmen, policemen, the warden, and even the governor! With those kinds of connections, if his brother would only meet with him, V was absolutely positive his plan would work. The arrangements for an absolute confidential meeting with Victor would have to be put into place. V was pretty sure of this, but first, he had to *convince* Victor to meet with him. Here lay the challenge. He thought, *Well, I guess Kevin will come and get me in a minute. He owes me, and now is the time to collect. Whether he likes it or not, he is part of this plan.*

While thinking about how he would manipulate Kevin, the cell door opened, and the light that flooded the room temporarily blinded V. A figure stood in the doorway, and V couldn't make out who it was.

"Kev, is that you, doc?"

"*Ohhh*, did you want to see your buddy Kevin? Sorry, dick face. I thought you'd be *glad* to see me. You don't *like* me, do you? Now that just hurts my feelings, and that's just too bad for your sake, that is."

It was Cooper.

"I was hoping you and I could be friends. I mean, we could *hang* out, if you know what I mean. Ha ha! Let me stop fucking with you. You and I both know I can't *stand* your ass! Come on, boy, let's get you back to your boyfriend Big Pussy." Cooper was grinning, looking just like a possum eating shit. He just didn't realize how ugly he really was. Or maybe he did. It didn't matter because all he knew was that he didn't like anyone that wasn't like him, and he definitely hated V. His hatred for V was more than racial but personal as well. He slapped the handcuffs and leg cuffs on V as tight as they could be placed on. V wanted to let out a small grunt in response to the pain, but as stated earlier, pain had become a familiar friend to him so he repressed it. It wouldn't be long now, except he still had to talk to Kevin to get the ball rolling. The walk back to his cell was no different from returning from a trip, and it seemed shorter. When he got there, the shackles were taken off, and he was pushed back inside his cell.

"Well, it looks like your *man*'s not here. Oh, *that's* right, it's mealtime. Guess you missed out on *that* too. Say, are you losing weight? That skin-and-bones look *fits* you. Ha ha! *Man*, I missed fucking with you! You miss *me*? What was that? You ain't got *nothing* to *say*? *Really*? You think you're tough *shit*, don't you? Oh well, every dog has his day. But remember that I am *your* master, and if you ever turn on me, I will shoot you between the goddamn eyes like the damned junkyard dog you are! You understand me, boy?"

V never responded. He just stared at the back wall of his cell. He had never been so focused in his life. Nothing Cooper could say or do at this point would stray him from his plans. V did, however, add something to his plans. He vowed that when he finished his business, he would find out where Cooper lived, go right up to his front door, and kick his racial, hateful ass. V heard the door slam and key turn as Cooper went away laughing. V turned to the cell and flipped Cooper off as if he were still there. Cooper was right about one thing: Every dog has his day, and the pit bull in V was about to come out.

CHAPTER 9

IMPLEMENTATION

Too much thought was given to Cooper. It was time to focus on the plan. Part A of V's master plan consisted of talking to Moms and seeing if she could convince Victor to come and meet with him. Part B of the plan was talking to Victor. Part C of the plan was proving his innocence, no matter what it took. That part hadn't really been worked completely out. *Oh yeah, I almost forgot part D—kick Cooper's ass!* thought V.

The inmates were just coming back from eating, and Kevin just happened to be bringing Big Percy and others to their perspective cells.

"Vincent!" Big Percy squealed. "You're back! Are you okay? You look thin. Don't worry, honey, I'm gonna nurse you back to health."

"No, thanks, Percy. Don't touch me, aw-ight?"

"Shit. If you say don't touch you, I *ain't* gon' fucking touch you. I saw what you did to Roger when he grabbed you. No *way*, honey. If I *do* nurse you, it will be with a ten-foot pole . . . that is, if you *want* to be nursed."

"Look, I don't have time to waste talking to you about this. We'll talk later *if* I feel like it. Right now, I gotta talk to Kev."

"*Damn*, honey, you ain't gotta bite my *head* off!" Big Percy got in his bed, turned his face to the wall, and began to sulk.

Big-ass baby! V thought. He saw Kevin walking by.

"Yo, Kev! Hold up! I gotta talk to you!"

"Let me finish my rounds. I'll be back in about twenty."

"I can't wait no damn twenty minutes! I need to talk to you *now*, man!"

"I'll tell you what, gadamnit, if you *really* need to talk to me, you *will* wait twenty minutes or *longer* if it takes that! When I finish what I have to do, I'll be back! Do you fucking understand *that*?" Kevin got a little agitated at V's arrogance.

"Aw-ight, man, I understand. Sorry 'bout that. You know where to find me."

* * *

Forty-five minutes passed before Kevin returned to talk to V.

"What up, Kev? You got a smoke?" V didn't even smoke before he was sentenced to death row, but when one is accused of murder, and he knows he didn't do it, one might find himself smoking a *lot*.

"So, V," Kevin asked while handing V a cigarette and lighting it, "what did you want to talk to me about? Seemed urgent, but you know I got a job to do first."

"I know. I need your help. Now I'm not *threatening* you, but I did see you and Big Percy pass some papers to each other a couple of weeks ago. I wonder what that could have been. Or do I already know? You know, the more I think about this, I guess I *am* threatening you. You want me to talk about what I know, or that could be known, to the warden, or are you ready to cooperate with me?"

"Hold your voice down, man! If I know *you*, you know more than you're saying. Okay, I'll help you. *Damn!* What do you want?" Kevin now lit a cigarette for himself to smoke. It seems like a cigarette has a calming effect on someone *not* on death row. Kevin had a pretty good job and didn't want to do anything to jeopardize it.

"First of all, I need you to arrange for me to talk to my mom . . . but in the strictest of confidence. Simple enough, right? Second of all, I need a room where I can meet with my brother . . . again, in the strictest of confidence. Third, and this is probably the most important . . ." V paused, looking over his shoulder for dramatic effect. He wanted Kevin to think that the last thing would require an extra effort.

"Third of all, on the lowest of down-low moves . . . I need a carton of Marlboro Lights Special Blend . . . shorts . . . in the strictest of confidence, of course." V was smiling at this point.

"Is that *all*?" Kevin was relieved that this was all V asked for, but he still feared that V wouldn't be quiet about his meeting with Big Percy.

"If I do all you ask, how can I be sure you'll keep your mouth shut about my 'transactions'?"

"You can't. You just have to trust me. Look in my eyes, man, and if I lie about what I'm about to say, or even if you *feel* like I'm lying, don't do it. It's as simple as that."

Kevin looked at Vincent deep in his eyes and nodded with agreement.

"Okay. Convince me," Kevin said.

"If you help me, your secret will go to the grave with me."

Kevin paused and thought about this statement and then nodded again. He was convinced that V was being truthful. Besides, his chances were better *helping* V than *not* helping him.

"But," V continued, "on the other hand, if you don't help me, your shit will be out in the streets and on the front page of the newspaper by Sunday. Do you fucking understand *that*?"

Since it was Wednesday, V thought that maybe he would keep this reminder first and foremost in Kevin's mind. Kevin smiled.

"Yeah, I understand. I can't have you fucking up my shit. It's too important. But you know what? I'll help you, but if any of *my* information gets out before I *want* it to get out, it may not be a secret, but your ass will be in the grave regardless. You know, you could just wind up dead *before* Sunday."

"No *shit*, Sherlock. But so could *you*. And besides," V continued, "my birthday is next month, and I plan on being *out* of this hole before then."

"Riiiight!" Kevin replied. He had just decided that helping V would not make much of a difference. He was on death row, and it was just a matter of time before they passed down a date of execution. He knew about V's brother Victor being one of the best defense attorneys in the country, but there was probably nothing that *he* could do to help to get V out of jail. Not after killing a judge. If he helped V, he knew that when the execution was finished, V had no choice but to take the "secret" to his grave. It's been over three years anyway, and it didn't look like Victor even cared.

"When do you want this done?" Kevin asked.

"*Yesterday*, doc. Yesterday . . . as in right *now*. It shouldn't take you more than an hour to put things in motion. I expect to see you soon with some good news. Right?"

After making his requests, V turned his back on Kevin as if to say that he had done all the talking he would do. It was now on Kevin's shoulders to bring about some action to the plan.

"Yeah. Right." Kevin left chuckling, trying not to look like he was in too much of a hurry. That is, until he was out of sight. He picked up the pace and got on the phone trying to reach V's mother. At this juncture, this was equally as important to him. The business transactions that he did in secret, he would like to keep them that way.

Big Percy sat up on his bed. He'd learned that when V was having a conversation with someone, *he* was not to be seen or heard. V wasn't a big man, but what he knew could kill a man with just one move. While Victor was studying his books, Vincent was experiencing life. He had been taught over the years and had become a black belt in tae kwon do and a brown belt in jiujitsu. Had he known that he would be jumped by six men when he first got to prison, he probably would've been more prepared. He *should've* been. It was just another lesson in life. V wished he had asked for another cigarette before Kevin left, but at least he felt confident that he was working on the plan. He just stared down at the floor and took his final drag on his smoke.

"Honey, are you all right?" Big Percy asked, interrupting V's empty thoughts.

"Huh? Oh yeah. But, Percy, the nineteenth of next month is my birthday. I'll be turning twenty-six, and I plan on being out of here. Not just this cell, mind you, but this entire facility. I plan on spending that day with my woman, pleasing her and being pleased. I'm going to ask her to be my wife, so if you have any ideas of you and I *ever* being *anything* other than cellmates, forget about it. We *could* never and *will* never be. Also, I would appreciate it if you would no longer call me 'honey.' My name is Vincent Lavell Taylor, and you can call me Vincent, Vince, or just plain V. But don't call me Vinny. I hate that shit. Okay, not really. My mom calls me that, so . . . now you *will* respect my wishes, or do I have to threaten you too? You will find yourself waking up dead."

"What? A person can't *wake up* dead, you know," Percy said.

"You *know* what the fuck I mean. The coroner will call it a natural death, but you'll be dead all the same. Do I make myself clear?"

The tears were running down Big Percy's face like someone slapped him. He nodded his hot-ironed, pressed head and then turned quickly toward the wall in his bed.

"I understand you perfectly." Percy sniffled. "But you're a big-ass *meanie* and a *bully!*"

V climbed up onto the top bunk, lay on his back, and shook his head.

"Aw, stop being such a *crybaby*! That's how I *feel*, aw-ight? I'll bet you probably weren't a faggot when you first got—"

"Gay!" Percy corrected.

"Aw-ight . . . sorry. *Gay*. You weren't gay when you first *got* here, *were* you? Hell, in my neighborhood growing up, if we knew someone was a fucking fa—I mean, gay, we would just kick his ass for being different. We were wrong in feeling that way and acting out on those feelings. It wasn't until I got older that I realized everyone *couldn't* be the same. As long as they kept their shit over there, I didn't care *what* they did. So all I'm saying to you is keep *your* shit over *there* and we won't have any problems. I don't have to be a part of your world if I don't *want* to. You just have to accept the fact that all we are in *here* are cellmates. All we are in this *world* are human beings. *See* where I'm coming from?"

Big Percy composed himself so that he could respond to V's comments.

"Well, *Vincent*, I *was* gay before I came here. I've always known that I like men. I may not have always been 'flaming,' as you like to call it, but I knew. Do you know *why* I'm here? I was a star linebacker in college, but I killed three of my teammates when they gave me a hard time after they found out I dated an offensive lineman from another school. I didn't feel like I had to take any of their bullshit, and now I don't have to anymore. I'll respect your wishes, V, but you should know that I have *always* respected you as a person, but you should also know that I could fuck you up too! I'm not *afraid* to kill, you know. Have you *ever* killed someone? Oh, that's *right*, you killed a judge, didn't you?"

"*Fuck* you, Percy! I ain't killed anyone! But I guarantee you that if you cross me, *you* will be the first!"

"*Mmph*. Tough talk," Percy said under his breath.

There was about two minutes of silence between the two before V spoke up again.

"Yo, Big Percy. You said that you didn't have to take those guys' bullshit anymore, right? How many years did you get for killing them?"

"Triple life."

"*Shit!* Well, I guess you showed *them*, huh? Why are *you* not on death row?"

"Even though my lawyer showed that I was emotionally distracted and proved it to be self-defense, the judge just couldn't let me walk. So I'll die in prison but not the death row path."

"Damn, man. Well, I'll say this: Retaliation against another human being for wronging you and then getting a prison term because of your actions proved what? Life is a trip, Percy, but it surely should be spent *outside* of prison. And that's where *I* intend to be—on the *outside*!"

CHAPTER 10

BROTHER TO BROTHER

"Hello?"
"Hello, Moms? Hey, this is Vincent."
"Vincent! What a nice surprise! *How* were you able to call me?"
"You know how persuasive I can be. Ha ha!"
"Ha! Yeah, I guess you're right. How are you *doing*, baby?"
"I'm good. How about yourself?"
"I'm doing fine, sugar. Just fine. I *miss* you. Are they treating you okay? You know what? Don't answer that. I might not like your answer."
"Come on, Moms, they don't care *nothing* about me in here. But like I told you before, you don't have to worry about me. Just worry about your health. I'm cool. But I *did* call for a specific reason. Have you seen Vic?"
"Victor? Yes, I have. As a matter of fact, he's over here right now. He just got back in town from *somewhere*. He don't tell me much. *He did give me some money though,*" Moms whispered. She knew Victor liked to flaunt his good fortunes, but he didn't want V to know when he did something for Moms.
"Well, *that's* got to be a good thing, huh? Look, Moms, I *really* need to talk to Vic. Not just on the phone but in person too. I need you to convince him to come see me. Just one time. We both know he's the best lawyer in the country, and if he came and talked to me, I believe that, together, we could come up with something that would get me out of this place. I know you want that, *don't* you? Do you think you can help me, Moms?"
Moms's heartstrings were being pulled on, and she was especially a softie for her boys.

46

"Honey, you know that I'll do anything for you, but you also know that Victor is not that crazy about you. I don't know why though. Okay, *maybe* I know why. Anyway, you know how stubborn he is. I'll tell you what, though, when we get off the phone, and he leaves to go home, I'll call Terri, and maybe, together, we can goad him to come see you. Do you have some sort of plan?" Moms asked.

"What do you *think*? Yeah, Moms, I have a plan. Sorry if that seemed blunt." V couldn't take the chance that Moms and Terri wouldn't be able to change Victor's heart, so he had to take action.

"I understand, honey. You're under a lot of pressure."

"Yeah, I am. Say, Moms, put Vic on the phone, but don't tell him who it is. Just put him on, okay?"

"Okay, baby . . . Victor!" Moms yelled out to the other room. Victor was in the kitchen fixing himself a ham-and-cheese sandwich and some Kool-Aid, the "red" flavor. He wanted people to think that when he became successful, he had higher tastes and more class, but in reality, he couldn't resist eating a homemade lunch at his mom's with some red Kool-Aid.

"Victor! Telephone!"

Victor entered the room with a plate containing a sandwich, chips, and a large dill pickle. He used an empty washed-out mayonnaise jar to hold his iced-down drink. Classy!

"Who is it?" he asked. Victor always wanted to know who he was speaking with before he got on a phone just in case he needed to keep the upper hand in the conversation.

"It's for you" was all Moms gave him. She smiled when she said it, trying to make Victor less apprehensive about taking the call. She tried to make him think that maybe it was a female. He sat down his lunch and took the receiver.

"Hello. Victor Taylor. It's your dime, but it's my time."

"Hey, Vic! It's me, V. Don't hang up, aw-ight?"

"What the fuck! How were you able to make a phone call?"

V knew he had to talk fast, and he had to be convincing. *This may the last and only chance I get*, he thought.

"Listen up, brother. You know I'm on death row, and I know you probably couldn't be happier. I think I know a way to get off, but I need your help. I need to *see* you, man!"

"You'd be doing the world a favor if you were gone. Why should I help your punk ass get out?"

Moms had been eavesdropping but decided to let Victor have his "privacy," so as she stepped out of the room, she thought, *Because he's your brother.*

Victor was getting upset that V was keeping him from his lunch.

Think fast, man! Okay, here goes.

"Look, man, whether you like it or not, I'm your brother. I wish we had a better relationship, but we don't. Before you decide whether to meet with me or not, I'd like to say something. You remember all the times that I perpetrated you? Well, man . . ." V was going for the dramatic effect again, the way Moms would.

"Well, what, V?" Victor bit into his sandwich and made a smacking noise in the phone.

"Well, Vic, I fucked up, and I'm sorry. I never meant for any of my shit to get you into any kind of trouble. I was just having fun, but I guess it wasn't much fun for you. All I want to say is that I apologize and I was wrong for doing that to you."

Victor was dumbstruck. V had *never* apologized for *anything* he had done to his brother. Victor stopped chewing and smacking and began thinking about how important he was to *everyone* in his life. He now had his brother begging him for help. He loved the feeling of being the one who had the power to change a situation. V even said he was wrong, and in Victor's mind, if V was wrong, that made Victor right. Inside, he was as giggly as a kid in a candy store. He tried to hide his enthusiasm when he spoke again, so he swallowed what he had in his mouth and tried not to smile when he spoke.

"I have a couple of questions for you first, V," Victor said.

Shit! thought V. He hadn't anticipated questions. Maybe if he were silent, Victor would just go ahead and ask his questions. He was afraid that if he talked now, his voice would probably crack. Victor began.

"First off, when would you want to meet?" Victor asked.

"Well, today is Thursday, and I know how busy you are, so I was thinking maybe Saturday? That's the typical day for visits, you know. Say about, um, ten o'clock in the morning?"

"Naw, that won't work for me." Victor paused for a minute. "How about eleven instead? I've got something to do before then."

Victor didn't really have anything planned. He just had to give the impression that it was *he* was in control and called all the shots.

"Yeah, okay. I guess that's cool." V didn't really care *what* time they met. Showing up was all that mattered at this point.

"Okay then," Victor continued, "what's in this for me? You don't have any *money*, do you? You see, I get paid by the hour, and I figure I'll spend about an hour with you. That's about $750. I mean, the way I see it, you really can't offer me anything, can you? My time is precious . . . and expensive. What you got?"

"Oh sure, I have something. What's in it for *you* is that if you can help me to get out of here, I will leave town for good. Hell, maybe even the country. I'll never bother you again, and you will never see me again. We can even put it in writing. *You'll* have to set that up though."

Even though V didn't anticipate any questions, he already knew the answer to these. He also knew that if he did leave "for good," it would break Moms's heart. Right now, he just needed verbal leverage to move Victor. Hell, if enough money was involved, it might be worth the pain.

"You would *leave*? For *good*? Now *that*, my brother, is worth *more* than money to me! But let me say this: I make no promises of being able to get you out. But if I *can* get you out, then it will be up to you to get the hell out! Of town, that is. You know? Now that I *think* about it, I could probably put some papers together for you to leave the country. Now *that* would be the shit!"

"Okay, don't worry about that. If you just show up at eleven, *I'll* get me out," V responded.

"You seem mighty confident about this, and you have *surely* piqued my curiosity. Brother, I will most *definitely* be there, but I'll need a completely confidential atmosphere. We don't need any spectators, understand?"

Damn, this is working out better than I thought! V thought to himself.

"I totally agree, and I'm already working on that. Now, Victor, you *are* going to be here Saturday morning, right? Don't make me come looking for you!"

The brothers shared a rare laugh on that statement.

"Oh yeah, V. I wouldn't miss *this* opportunity for the world."

"Cool. And thanks, man. Say, can I talk back to Moms?"

"Yeah, hold on . . . Moms!" he called out, thinking that Moms was on the other side of the house, but she was standing right outside the doorway, listening to every word Victor said. She stepped in the room with teary eyes and gave Victor a big hug and a kiss on his cheek. She could not believe she was witnessing, as far as *she* was concerned, nothing short of a miracle.

"Thank you, Victor. God's gonna bless you real good for this," she said to her son.

"Yeah. Yeah, whatever. I'm already blessed, don't you think? I'm going, but he won't get out. Too much damn evidence."

He handed her the phone with a smug look on his face, mainly because of what he knew he *wouldn't* do for Vincent. He *would*, however, get that paperwork together for him to leave the country . . . just in case. He gathered up his lunch and headed to the den to watch TV.

"Hello."

"Hey, Moms. Well, I guess you heard, huh?"

"Yeah, baby. Leave the country if you get out? Did I hear that right?"

"Yeah, you heard right. I had to tell him something that he wanted to hear. You understand, don't you?"

"I guess so. I ain't gonna worry about that right now. I am just so happy and so proud of Victor for swallowing his pride to help you."

"Yeah. It's great, right? Say, Moms, have you seen or heard from Cassie or Junior?"

"I haven't heard from Cassie in a couple of days, but you and Junior must have some sort of ESPN. He called today. Sorry I forgot to tell you, I was just so excited and surprised to hear from you. Anyway, I told him what was going on with the solitary stuff, and he said he would cut his vacation short and head home as fast as he could to be here for you. He might make it in on Sunday or Monday. At least that's what he said."

V got quiet.

"Vince, are you still there?"

V's mind had wandered to thoughts of Cassie. He was filled with doubt, fear, and even a little rage. Doubt about him and her making it. Fear that she had found someone else. Rage that he was in jail instead of with her. Now he regretted *ever* being in trouble. She should have been his focus, but sometimes he would rather run around with his homeboy Junior. V thought Cassie was into thugs, so he tried to play up hard. To think of Cassie with another man was eating away into his heart.

"Vincent?"

"Oh yeah, Moms, I'm still here. Thanks for everything. When I get out of here, I'm going to do something real nice for you."

"You're a sweetie. Keep praying, dear. Prayer changes things. I saw that today."

"Okay, Moms. Oh, and, Moms? The word is ESP, not the sports channel, ESPN. Talk to you soon. Love ya."

"That's what I said, isn't it? Anyway, I love you too, sweetie. Bye, bye."

As they hung up, V's heart was heavy. He looked over at Kevin, who was standing by and gave him a nod. One half of his plan was carried out, and it seemed to go much smoother than he thought it would. V's shirt was stained with sweat around his neck and under his arms, mainly from the stress of the phone call. But hey, Victor Taylor, attorney at law, would be here on Saturday. For sure. Just *believing* this to be true raised V's spirits. As he was escorted back to his cell, V grilled Kevin on the final details of his plan: carton of cigarettes, confidential room, specific times, etc. Everything had to go off without a hitch. Kevin assured him that the cigs would be delivered tomorrow and the room would be ready for Saturday. V still bummed three cigarettes and some matches from Kevin before he left him. The sound of the cell door closing behind him and the clinking keys as they locked it were sounds that V felt he would not have to hear for much longer. Big Percy was asleep, so he didn't worry about being bothered by him. He climbed into his bunk with a pad and pencil and began doodling. He had been in prison enough times to know *never* write down plans or ideas. *Always* keep them in your head where no one can get to them, unless your mind is weak, that is. Moms had just told him to keep praying, but he didn't feel the need to pray because Moms was praying enough for the *both* of them. But she just might be right about one thing: Prayer might just change things. Come Saturday.

CHAPTER 11

SLAVERY

Kevin Casey had just finished his tour for the day and could think of nothing more than just going home and getting into bed. He was tired, mentally and physically. He was also a little tense, so he knew he had to take a shower first. The water was hot and seemed to wash away some of his worries and bust some of those stress bubbles off his back. *How the hell does he think he can threaten me?* These thoughts were about V. *He* really *doesn't know who I am! Boy! If only he did!* Kevin liked his job, didn't love it. He cared about his woman Debra, and he was okay with the way things were going in his life, all except for his daughter. He hadn't seen her in *years*. Sure he could probably get another job, but he would lose all the benefits he had acquired while working for the penal system, and he would be looked upon as dishonest. He could lose his woman, but then it wouldn't be the first time. He'd already been married before, and because of "irreconcilable differences," things just didn't work out between them. He personally brought too much baggage into the relationship that neither one of them could unpack. He was a dreamer, and she was a realist. It certainly didn't help the relationship. His only regret was when she left, she took his daughter with her and fixed it so he could not have visitation rights or even *see* her. It had been seventeen years since he last laid eyes on her, and he didn't even know where she might be, what happened in her life, or if she was even still *alive*. He missed her, and work was one of the things that kept his mind preoccupied. He had ideas and plans, but he needed a few key people to help him to pop them off. Debra helped, but she was just a woman. Not being negative, it's just that Kevin thought that he should be the sole provider and his woman should do anything she wanted or nothing she didn't. Even though he cared for Debra, she was not his first wife, whom he still had love for. His daughter still had his heart, and no one could ever replace the feelings he had for her. He didn't know if Debra could be his soul mate, and since his first wife didn't turn out to be his soul mate, maybe he wasn't supposed to have one. Without a doubt, he was certainly glad that she was in his life and supported his dreams. She was allowing him to be the knight in shining armor, and he was determined to deliver.

He stepped out of the shower, and after drying off, he wrapped the towel around his waist as he made it to his locker.

"Officer Casey! So it's *not* true what they say about your kind!"

Cooper had just entered and wanted to cause some static.

"What the hell is *that*, Coop?" Kevin didn't like Cooper, just about as much as the inmates. There were only a handful of people who actually did. Cooper didn't care. He had a reputation of pissing people off just for the fun of it.

"They say you don't wash yourselves very good, but you smell like roses in springtime, and you do realize that if you smell a rose up close, it smells like shit, right?"

"You kiss my hairy black ass, Coop! And get the fuck out of my way!"

Cooper stepped aside to let Kevin pass but sniffed on his shoulder as he did. Kevin whirled around and threw a punch that landed squarely on Cooper's skinny bicep. Cooper grabbed his arm, which now throbbed with pain, bent over, and spat at Kevin's feet. He's lucky he missed.

"You black-assed fool!" Cooper said, trying to hold back a tear. That punch *hurt*. He went over to his own locker and opened it up to show a full-length picture of that year's Playboy Bunny, all the while rubbing his arm.

"Look, *I* didn't start this shit. *You* did," Kevin said. "I guarantee you this though: I *will* finish it. Did it ever occur to you that if you didn't piss people off *all* the fucking time, you might have a friend or two?"

Now *Kevin* was grinning. He *knew* he hurt Cooper with that punch and was proud of it. If anyone deserved to be a human punching bag, it was Cooper.

"A friend or two, huh? Like you and some of your inmate friends? Like, um, let's see now . . . Big Percy? Pee Wee? That snake, Vincent Taylor? That sorry son of a—"

"Look, Coop, I know that you hate the man for *supposedly* killing the judge, but he claims he's innocent. What if, by chance, he *didn't* kill him? If it were proven that he didn't do it, would you forgive and forget?" Kevin asked, almost as if he was asking the question to himself. At first, Kevin thought his *own* secret was out. He just hoped Cooper couldn't see how hard his heart was beating.

"Oh, he killed him, all right. It's because of people like him that I have *fewer* friends. You know, the friends I do have seem to stop living. The only thing is they don't always have the choice of whether to live or die. It doesn't matter though. Vincent's done *something* in his life he's probably gotten away with. This is just poetic justice."

"You mean to tell me that if all a man did was *steal* some stuff, he *deserves* the *death penalty*? What kind of sense does *that* make?"

The more Kevin talked about it, the more he started to believe that maybe Vincent *was* innocent. He thought, *Come to think of it, why would V try so hard to prove his innocence if he was truly guilty? Most inmates, who are guilty, try to prove how hard and tough they are in prison rather than how innocent they are. They just accept the time they have left or accept their death sentence, even if they are not ready to spend the rest of their lives behind bars or die. That is, unless V just didn't want to die, period.*

Cooper was changing from his guard clothes into to his rebel flag T-shirt and old raggedy jeans. Country boy at heart . . . if he had a heart.

"It *doesn't* make any sense," Cooper said. "Stealing is one thing, but we're not talking about thievery, are we? We're talking *murder*! A man was found dead! My friend! And if there were fingerprints all over the murder weapon that killed the judge or *any* man, why should the state set the owner of those prints free? You know all about evidence. If *you* were on the jury, how would you have pleaded? Would *you* have given a not guilty verdict?" Cooper asked with conviction and a stern look.

Kevin knew that what Cooper said made as much or more sense as anything *he* had just said. Evidence is always hard to overrule.

"No. No, I guess I wouldn't."

Kevin had to swallow his pride. He had just had a battle a wits or rather, common sense, with Cooper, and lost. He was just grateful that this conversation had been an A-to-B one and there was no one there to C the outcome.

"No, I didn't *think* so. So Mr. Vincent Taylor's little stay here has not been and *won't* be a pleasant one. Leading up to the date of execution, whenever that is, he will have *plenty* to deal with, and someone is making damn sure of that!" Cooper grinned, while tapping on a small notebook.

"What do you mean by that? Do you know something no one else knows?"

Kevin was fully dressed by now and walking over to Cooper's locker. Cooper's grin disappeared from his face because he knew he had said and shown too much. He also knew that Kevin wasn't going to leave the issue alone. All he really knew was that he didn't want Kevin to hit him with those big soup bone hands again.

"Let me see that!" Kevin said.

Cooper tried to hide the notebook behind his back.

"No, gaddamnit!" Cooper found himself saying with boldness he should not have had at this very instance.

Kevin raised his fist to hit Cooper, and Cooper knew from a very recent experience that his aim was true.

"Okay, *okay*! *Shit!* You may be sorry for seeing this, but I guess a *bought* lesson is the only kind you'll understand."

Kevin looked at the notebook and saw a list of items and instructions dealing with the treatment of V. He was shocked to see where an inmate was to reach around V, *knowing* that V would react the way he did. Even the part about six guys jumping him as soon as he got there! Everything was staged, and V was getting set up and didn't even know it. What they didn't know, however, was how *tough* V really was. Even more shocking was the upcoming, planned, detailed treatments to come.

"I guess you or *whoever* is pulling your strings didn't count on *me* being there when some of this shit happened, did you?" Kevin asked.

"Nope, but it only prolongs the agony, don't you *think*? And besides, you can't be there *all* the damn time, *can* you? Like now. What's happening right now, Casey?"

"Stop all that goddamn grinning. Tell me, who's behind this? I mean, do you really *believe* you can get away with this?"

Cooper rubbed his arm and offered Kevin a cigarette. Without thinking, he took it and lit it.

"Who's gonna stop us? *You?* Shiiiittt! *That's* a fucking joke, if I *ever* heard one. You can't stop us because you don't know who *us* is! I'm just one of *many*. Or a few. Who knows? I answer to someone who answers to someone, and then there's one big honcho over the whole thing. I don't know who it is, but if I had to guess, it would be that Sabino guy. Hell, we could *kill* Vincent . . . if we wanted to. I just know that if I do that, I wouldn't be following orders, and I could just be another dead red neck, as you call me. Matter of fact, we could kill *your* black ass or anyone else we choose, but like I told my 'benefactors,' I personally like to see people suffer. Especially blacks. Sorry, but I'm not sorry. But most of all, as 'you people' say, it's all about the *Benjamins!*"

Cooper knew now what he would do. Kevin would now have to be on "payroll" . . . without a choice and without pay. Pick that cotton, lift that bale. Free slavery in the twentieth-century.

"You see, Officer Casey, curiosity really *does* kill the cat. And since you just *had* to see my notebook, you now work for *me, without* payment, that is. You *will* do what I say, or I will make sure you never see your daughter again. How old is she now, twenty-one, twenty-two?"

"How do you know about my . . . ? Don't you *fuck* with my daughter!" Kevin said with a firm grip of Cooper's shirt.

"Naw. Don't you fuck with *us*! If you *really* want her to stay alive, you will let me go and do as you're told. Can you dig *that* . . . *brother?*"

Cooper flashed his possum grin. Kevin released the shirt with a push attached. V had Kevin where he knew he *needed* him. Cooper now had Kevin where he thought he *wanted* him. There was nothing Kevin could do now but what he was instructed to do. Yessuh, Massa.

CHAPTER 12

LOVELY SCENERY

The ride back to New York from New Orleans was a colorful one, filled with acres of farmland and flowers. The leaves were a mixture of gold, red, and brown with the occasional green from the trees that never change. Junior always liked to take the scenic route, but this time he didn't stop and take in any of the sights like he usually did. He had a very important reason for hurrying home. His boy V was locked up and probably needed some help with some plan. Junior was always willing and available to help out with a plan to get him, V, or both of them, out of trouble. V was the brains; Junior was the man of action. Whatever they put their heads together on came to fruition. This time, though, Junior was sure that V was going through a personal hell and in the dark about what type of action to take. With no one to put the plan into action, it was like V was in a no-win situation. The only thing Junior knew for certain was that he had to hurry home to help out any way he could. This trip was different in another way as well. Junior had a traveling companion, a female one. He wasn't quite sure how his best friend would take this, but this particular female was the one Junior was in love with, and there was nothing anyone could do about it. Besides, V *had* a girlfriend. Why couldn't Junior? Did he *mean* to fall in love? No way! There's an old saying that says a person can fall in love at first sight. In Junior's case, that is exactly what happened. She looked at him, batted those beautiful big light brown eyes and said, "You're sitting in my *seat*, sugar." He had to compose himself before he got up, or else, he would have fallen to the floor.

"Oh, is this *your* seat? I am sooo sorry," he said while holding the chair for her as she sat down. That's all it took; he was stricken. He had to get to know her better, but little did he know that the feelings he had for her now she would eventually have for him. That's the very reason why she teased him the way she did. *She* wanted to know *him* as well. They've been together for the past three months, and he thought he would share the good news with his ace. Even though he wasn't looking, he felt he finally found "the one." He would always come home with a bit of luck in his pockets, mostly financial luck. But this time he didn't feel lucky because of this girl; he felt blessed. Luck comes by chance; blessings come from God. Her name was Patricia, and he *loved* her. It was strange for him to feel this way about just *one* woman, and even stranger for him was the love itself. He had always hit it and quit it in the past. He knew the type to hook up with. They seemed to want the same thing he did: a good night with a good lover but no commitments. They were clean health-wise, but when it came to sex, they had to get a little "something, something" too. Patricia was different. She had class and a sense of style and flair unmatched by any woman Junior had ever met. However, she wasn't stuck-up and could easily fit in with any group of people. Junior couldn't stand to be around girls who walked around with their noses in the air and looked down on anyone not driving a Bentley or didn't make a six-figure income. They were flakier than a Hungry Jack biscuit. He liked the kind of girls that liked to do some of the things he liked but also strong enough mentally to make their own decisions, especially if they really didn't want to do something just to make someone else happy. They had to have their heads on straight and know what they wanted out of life. They had to stimulate him mentally with intelligent conversation. They had to be beautiful on the inside. Patricia fit all the criteria, and her being fine and beautiful on the outside didn't hurt. The real question for the both of them was, can this really be a love in which they can make a lifelong commitment?

"Hey, baby, can we stop at the rest area coming up? I gotta pee!" Patricia said while rocking her legs together.

"Yeah, sure. I guess we should've stop at the last one, huh? My bad. I'm trying to get home ASAP, know what I mean? Damn, how come we can't find at least *one* good radio station in Pennsylvania? Man, I miss WJMS. They be jamming!"

"Really?" Patricia asked.

"Yeah, baby, I wouldn't lie to you about a serious thing like that."

"Bullshit." She coughed.

"Ha ha. You're funny. As a matter of fact, let's get Sirius radio when we get back. K?"

"K. I may be funny, but I know I gotta pee! And if I cough again, we won't even have to stop, and these seats will be stained."

Junior couldn't help but laugh as he pulled over into the rest area. He looked in his cup holder for some loose change for a couple of soft drinks.

"Hey, you want one?" he called out to Pat as she hurried to the bathroom.

"Yeah, DP, if you don't mind," she called back over her shoulder as she disappeared behind the women's bathroom door.

He headed for the Coke machine and purchased her a Dr. Pepper and himself a Coke. He thought to himself, *Man, she's nice! I wonder if Moms would like her. Well, even if she doesn't, it won't affect the way I feel about her. She's got a nice ass too! Yep, yep!*

Junior hoped that V didn't think he abandoned him. Had he known earlier that V was in trouble in jail, he would've dropped everything and come home right away. But then he would not have gotten to know Patricia the way he had. She was special in his eyes, but he hoped the time spent with her didn't cost him his friend's life and, if he *was* still alive, his friend's trust.

Patricia came out of the restroom and saw him standing beside the Coke machine, taking a few sips from his bottle. She headed his way, smiling a smile which had "mischievous" written all over it. She came up to him, grabbed the unopened bottle of Dr. Pepper in one hand, and reached down with the other hand to give his "member" a slight squeeze.

"Thank you, baby. You're so *sweet*!" she said as she took her drink. To Junior, it sounded like she sang the words.

"No, thank *you*! But now *I've* got to go pee!"

Patricia had tried to do this on the sly, but an elderly couple was sitting on one of the rest area benches, and the old man saw the whole scene. He may have been an older man, but he wasn't blind, and he wasn't dead. The old man had feelings of arousal that he hadn't had for the past five years. He grabbed his wife by the hand, and they headed for their car.

"Where are we going?" the old woman asked her husband.

"We're going to check into that Holiday Inn off the freeway."

"What for?"

"For a little 'afternoon delight,' if you get my drift."

"Hell, boy, if I thought you were serious, I would have dragged *you* to the car. Oh well, I know that once we get in the room, you're going to sleep. It's a good thing it's time for your nap anyway."

"Oh yeah?"

"Yeah!"

The old man stopped dead in his tracks and looked at his wife deep in her eyes.

"Okay, I guess you're right. I *am* sleepy," he said.

"I know, I know. But I still love you," she said.

Junior came out the men's restroom, cheesing because he saw the old man witness Patricia's sensual touch. Junior liked the fact that she would play with him in public. Junior walked over to Patricia and whispered in her ear the fact that she had been busted. She spewed out the swallow of drink in her mouth, which gave Junior a good laugh.

"You ready to hit the road, Pat?" he asked, trying not to sound like he was rushing her, but he knew he had to get a move on now. V might need him, and Junior was ready to help.

"I'm *ready* when *you're* ready, sweet thing," she said with a sexual overtone.

This *really* made Junior cheese. He liked Patricia, but he knew she would not deter him from getting to his friend. She would just bide her time until they got settled, and then it was *on*. She noticed the rise in Junior's pants from all the teasing and thought maybe she should do something to get him back on track.

"You know what?" she asked. "Vincent is probably waiting for you, and we'll *never* get where we're going if you're just going to stand there with a woody. Unless you plan on *driving* with that thing."

"Yeah, you're right. Down boy, down! You need to stop teasing me, baby," Junior playfully said.

"Oh, I'm not teasing. I'm setting you up for promises."

"Aw *shit*, then let's hit it!"

With Pat by his side, he jumped behind the wheel of the BMW 315i, which actually belonged to her, and sped down the freeway. He left his car back in Louisiana, but he still couldn't believe she would offer not only to take the trip with him, but also suggested they take her car. *Hmmm*. Makes a brother think. Anyway, Junior hoped V liked her as much as *he* did.

They had driven about five miles, content with the fact they were with each other, when Patricia broke the silence.

"So you and Vincent are pretty tight, huh?"

"Man, V and I are like brothers! By the way, you can call him V. Everyone does. Did I ever tell you he had a twin? Identical! *I* should have been his *real* brother instead of the funky-ass one he has. And he's a lawyer too."

"*What? Vincent's* a *lawyer?* I mean, V's a lawyer?"

"Naw, his brother Victor. *One* of the best, if not *the* best in the country. Anyway, do you know he won't even *help* his brother? Can you *believe* that shit?"

"How do *you* know he won't help?"

"V's mom told me. We call her Moms, so that's what *you* have to call her. Anyone that is a friend of her sons, or a friend of mine, calls her Moms. Come to think of it, just about *everybody* calls her Moms. She's just this sweet person, and it feels like she's really your mother."

"She *sounds* nice."

"Oh, she *is*. Trust me."

"Baby, I *do* trust you. Love you too."

"Oh, it's like *that*, is it? Well, you're not the *only* one!"

"I already *know* you love yourself."

"You're silly. I do love myself, but what I meant was that I love you too."

Patricia smiled and leaned back in the seat and closed her eyes.

Junior missed Moms. She took to him as if he really was her own son. It was almost like she was missing someone in her life, and Junior filled the void. Junior was eleven when he lost both of his parents in a car accident, and he had to stay with his aunt Jenny. Jenny was married to an army officer who was stationed at three different military installments before retiring in New York. Junior was just starting his junior year in high school when he met Victor and Vincent, and he and V became the closest of friends. Junior took to Moms, and she became a source of inspiration that he needed in his life. His uncle never said anything of substance for Junior, just military talk and talk of the military. It was all his uncle knew. Uncle Marcus would have loved nothing more than for his nephew to join some sort of armed forces, preferably the army, and become an officer like he had done. Even though Junior didn't see that as something he wanted to do, his uncle still kept Junior out of trouble and helped mold him into a respectable young man. Moms, however, gave Junior a different perspective.

Moms would say, "Honey, if you just put your mind to it, there is *nothing* you can't do and no one you can't become. Don't let *anyone* else determine who you are *supposed* to be or what you are supposed to *do*. Just remember, it's *all* up to you. *You* are the ruler of your destiny, but always remember that God is in control."

She was more than right. Junior may have conned a few people in his life for a small financial gain, and he surely was no saint, but he had accomplished *every* goal that he shot for. If it weren't for Moms, he probably would not have attempted to find his true purpose in life. He got a little teary-eyed thinking of the influence Moms had on him. He looked over at Patricia and smiled, thinking how she and Moms would hit it off. She must have sensed his looking at her because she opened her eyes to catch him doing so.

"What you thinking about, baby?" Patricia asked.

"Oh, just a couple of women I love." He winked at her.

Patricia smiled and winked back just before dozing off.

CHAPTER 13

D-Day

Saturday morning was finally here, and V was a little tense about it coming so fast. Excited but tense all the same. It was just not that the day had come, he began to doubt if his plan would work, and he *never* doubted himself before. He knew he had about four hours before Victor would come to visit and hoped that was enough time to calm his nerves.

Who the hell am I trying to fool? I know the closer it gets to the meeting, the worse it will get!

V was on his way to the mess hall when Cooper saw him and started in on him.

"Well, look who's coming to dinner, boys. It's Mr. Vincent D. Taylor!"

"There's no D in my name, Cooper, but at least you got the 'Mr.' part right," V responded.

"Oh, sorry about that, sir," Cooper chimed back. "I thought the D stood for dog shit!" Cooper laughed while nudging Kevin with his elbow. Kevin gave Coop a weak smile.

V knew if he didn't at least respond to Cooper's comments, it would look suspicious. He walked on by both Cooper and Kevin but not without giving a look to Kevin as if to say "What are you doing with him?" Kevin couldn't even look back to V, and this gave V an uneasy feeling. Was Kevin going back on his word? V hoped not. It just wasn't like Kevin to hang out with the enemy and not look at his friends. But then again, was V really one of his friends? Or were who V thought were *his* friends really *his* enemies?

Hell, he's just working. That's all. He's just doing what he is paid to do. Ain't no shit.

As V sat down to eat, Pee Wee, one of his fellow inmates, sat down in front of him biting into a piece of bacon. He wasn't any taller than five feet, but for some reason or another, no one messed with him either.

"Say, V! Man, I understand that you're going to talk to your brother today, man!"

Damn!

"How did you find out about that, Pee Wee? No one was supposed to know about this! Damn!"

"Shhh, man! Don't nobody know about this shit but *me*, and I have my ways of finding out important shit like this. Shit that I can use for my *own* advantages. Know what I mean, man? Don't ask me for my sources 'cause I ain't telling you shit! But if you don't hold your loud-ass voice down, everybody *else* in this joint is gonna know."

V wanted to reach across the table and grab this little runt and force him to tell where he got the info, but he knew Cooper had his eye on him and was just *waiting* for the opportunity of V slipping up. At this point, he *had* to play this boy's game.

"What do you expect to gain from this information? I mean, how does this benefit you?"

"Well, man, *when* you do talk to your brother, I was thinking you might want to put in a good word for me. You see, man, you may not believe this, but your brother is the main holdup for me getting out of here. He's slow-poking. He knows *me*!"

"*Really?* He's holding *me* up too."

"Well, man, I may be of some service to you . . . that is, if I was *out* of this place. I know some things about the judge's murder, man."

"You *do*? *What* things? Bitch, you tell me!" V asked, trying to stay out of earshot of anyone.

"Look, man, what do you take me for, some kind of Willy bubble gum? My name's Pee Wee, man, not Boo Boo the fool! So if you want the info *I* have, I gotta be outta this motherfucker! Dig? And I ain't yo' *bitch*! Bitch!"

V looked straight in Pee Wee's eyes, and something told him that he was telling the truth.

"Look at it this way, man. I must be someone special or at least *know* someone special to be the only one in this prison that knows things that could help you. Hell, I know about your meeting, don't I? So look, when you meet with your brother, you tell your brother to call the warden and say these words: Free Pee Wee Sea . . . in question form."

"Yeah, I see."

"Naw, dumbass, I wasn't asking you if you *saw*. I was *telling* you. The phrase is 'Free Pee Wee Sea.' Like the ocean. But you gotta ask it in question form. I know you're not stupid, but I have been wrong before."

V let this wisecrack roll off his back and made the decision to go ahead and take a chance on Pee Wee. He really didn't have anything to lose, and Pee Wee just might have some info that could make a difference.

"So what, are you undercover or something? Never mind. You don't have to answer that. If you tell me, you'll have to kill me, right? Ha! Okay, Pee Wee. I'll put in a good word for you. But if this shit gets you out, you better look me up in a hurry. You don't want me to come looking for you. Aw-ight, man?"

V was serious.

"That's cool, man, but you don't have to put in a good word for me. Just say the words I *told* you to say. As soon as I'm out, expect to hear from me, say, in about a week after that. But if I *don't* get out, well, man . . . it was nice knowing your ass."

Pee Wee got up from the table and headed out of the mess hall and back to his cell. He grinned as he walked past Cooper and Kevin, which made them look past him and straight to where V was. He looked up from the table and met their eyes with a flip of his head as to say "What's up?" He got up, disposed of his tray, and headed out, making sure he looked at Kevin.

Did this motherfucker betray me? If he was smart, he didn't.

Kevin finally looked up, long enough to wink at V without Cooper noticing. This helped put V's mind at a little ease but not totally. Now his thoughts shifted to his brother Victor. *Is he really coming? If he does, is he going to help or just gloat? Hell, what if he does? Doesn't matter. Just as long as his ass shows up, we'll work this out.* V knew if he didn't concentrate on what to say and how to say it just right, he would ruin all his chances of freedom. He would only get this one move, one blow at meeting with his brother.

* * *

Victor had just gotten out of his Jacuzzi and was heading through the patio doors that were right outside the kitchen. He thought he take a swim in his Olympic-sized heated pool but decided a nice whirlpool would relax him better. It was nice to have an indoor pool because it was actually cold outside. He had the finer things in life, but he did not want any servants. Having servants would mean he would have to pay someone *some* of his money, and he wasn't having any of that. His *wife* could clean up what needed cleaning. He turned off the eggs he had boiling on the stove and put a couple of slices of toast in the toaster. Victor was about to have a sit-down with his brother Vincent. D-day! Victor decided that whatever V's plans were, he would not do *anything* to help. Well, *maybe* he would. He did have some paperwork for V to sign that forces him to move out of the country. *If V agrees to this, I'll make sure all provisions are taken care of.* Terri came downstairs and disturbed Victor's train of thought.

"I swear, Victor, you could have at *least* grabbed a robe!"

Victor was buck naked in the kitchen, and Terri was upset with him because he said he didn't feel like making love last night. Or this morning. He said there was too much on his mind, and it wouldn't be fair to either of them. The *real* reason was that as much as possible, he attempted to abstain from sex with his wife when *she* initiated it. He thought this must be the time she was ovulating, and he <u>did</u> <u>not</u> want any children.

"Look, Terri, I'm at home. I can do what I *damn* well please, thank you very much! And if I want to walk around my own damn house with my ass out, then I will! Shit!"

"Whatever," she replied.

Terri went to the refrigerator and grabbed the orange juice. Victor went into the bathroom that was downstairs right beside the garage and the laundry room and grabbed a robe.

"Well, seeing as how you don't like to see me in my birthday suit anymore, I'll put on this robe just for you."

"It's not that I don't like *seeing* you in your birthday suit. I hardly *ever* see you in your birthday suit. Not the way I *want* to anyway."

Facing this reality really hurt Terri's feelings. She could sense something was wrong, and she started having a low self-esteem. She was fine as wine and just as beautiful on the inside as the outside. She knew she shouldn't let *any* man make her feel this way, but she couldn't help it.

She liked Victor. If only he were a better person or had a better attitude or treated her like, say, a *wife* or something. Victor could tell this was bothering her and thought maybe he should say *something*, something nice.

"I'm sorry, baby. Hey, look, after I take care of my meeting with Vincent, let me take you out to dinner this evening. You make all the arrangements."

Terri just stood there looking up at the ceiling, trying not to cry, blowing out deep breaths.

"What do you say, Terri? Can I make it up to you? Okay, lover? I'll even try to put all business aside and concentrate on you. Okay . . . *sweetheart?*" Victor said in his most romantic voice. It was fake, but she bought it.

"Okay."

"Great! Hey, look, I·gotta get dressed, but all I want you to do is get your hair done, your nails, get a massage—you know, the works! And think about where you want to go tonight, aw-ight?"

Although Victor was an acclaimed lawyer, the street slang came out every once in a while because of he and V switching places so much when they were younger. He gave Terri a long passionate kiss that made her wet between her legs. She had to face the facts: She was horny and *needed* some loving. But she *wasn't* ovulating. Not at this moment. She just wanted to be with her husband. The man that *said* he loved her but found it harder and harder to show it. Yes, he could be a complete asshole at times, but she still found him to be the most interesting and attractive man she had ever met. His strength with people was admirable, and his confident conversation, while rubbing most people the wrong way, was cute in her eyes. Terri got on the phone and started making arrangements to be a knockout when Victor returned home. Victor headed up the stairs to get dressed.

"Vic, I'm going to buy a new dress too. I've just about worn everything else I have. I want to be a knockout for you. Okay? I want tonight to be special."

"Go ahead, girl. And don't worry. After this Vincent fiasco, there will be much cause to celebrate. This whole *weekend* will be *unforgettable!*"

CHAPTER 14

DON'T I KNOW YOU?

"How are you doing today, Mr. Taylor?" Cooper asked Victor as Cooper opened the front gate to allow Victor passage in. Cooper had to be nice to him because he knew that Victor could make a phone call and not only have his job, but also his wife's *and* his two sons' jobs as well. He might even be able to put a hit on Cooper, but Victor had never done that to anyone and really didn't know if he could. The one thing Cooper hated so much was that Victor looked so much like Vincent it was uncanny. If Cooper had not just seen V in his cell, he would swear the man driving this expensive automobile just escaped from prison.

"I'm quite well, Officer. And you?" Victor asked in his proper legal voice.

"Better'n your brother," Cooper said before thinking. He even let out a small laugh and was smiling, but it dissolved when he was sure he had said the wrong thing. Victor just pulled down his shades just enough so Cooper could see his eyes.

"Yes, I bet you are," Victor said. He smiled and then drove on through to a parking space. Cooper called another guard to take his place for about ten minutes. He suddenly needed to take a piss and a smoke break.

When Victor finally got inside the prison facility, he was met by Kevin, who told him that once they reached the room he was escorting him to, his brother should be there shortly. He also informed Victor that he alone would be standing guard outside the room just in case of any problems.

"Just yell and I'll be right in."

Kevin opened the door to what looked like a room for the "crazies" who liked to throw themselves against the wall. Victor took a seat and asked if it was okay to smoke. Kevin pulled out his cigarettes and lighter and offered them to Victor. He accepted them thinking this would only save him from busting open his own pack. He lit the cigarette and handed the pack and the lighter back to Kevin. Kevin then stepped outside the door and waited for Vincent to arrive. It was 10:57 a.m., and Victor thought about what he would say to V to make him *think* he was trying to help him.

Hmm, this cigarette has a nice flavor to it. Maybe I'll switch, thought Victor as he took long drags on his fag. The door opened again, and V was brought in, shackled on his ankles and wrists. Once getting inside, Kevin looked at Vincent and pointed to his watch, unlocked the shackles, and carried them out with him as he closed and locked the door behind him. The time now was *exactly* 11:00 a.m.

"Victor," V said with no emotion.

"Vincent," Victor replied in the same tone.

The brothers couldn't be *too* cordial to each other. They were both feeling a lot of pain. One because of *portrayals* without consent, and the other because of *betrayals* without consideration. The *strange* thing was even after all the time they had been apart, it still was like looking into a mirror and seeing one's reflection. The familiarity was eerie but welcomed to a degree. They had forgotten just *how* much alike they looked. Except for the clothes, that is. V took the chair right across his brother.

"Damn, man, I am *so* glad you came. You're looking *good*, doc! *Seriously*," V said.

"You look like *shit*. *Seriously*."

Be cool, V. Just be cool, V thought.

"Say, dude, what's that cologne you have on? It smells *nice*, doc. Got a sample? I *know* you still keep your atomizer with you, am I *right*?"

V knew his brother *all* too well.

"Yeah, you're right. I *have* some. It's called Monte Blanc Legend Spirit. Who are *you* trying to impress? Your *boyfriend*?"

Victor was enjoying this. He reached into his blazer inside pocket and grabbed his cologne and handed it to V. He wouldn't help him get out, but he wouldn't deprive him of *smelling* nice. V flipped him off under the table.

"Thanks, Vic. Hey, do you remember the time we were riding in the car with Moms and we kept trying to get her to pass other cars on the freeway? She kept telling us she was going plenty fast enough. Remember? But we kept on and on until she finally passed a car doing about eighty," V recollected, laughing.

"Yeah, I remember," Vic replied, not laughing.

"Who knew she was passing an unmarked police car, huh? Man, she whipped our asses good when we got home. Hee hee."

"Yeah, that may be funny *now*, but it hurt then, didn't it?" Vic replied.

"Yes, it did. Hey, remember the time we were going to surprise Moms on her birthday and Dad came home early? We thought it was her, so we jumped out from behind the couch and shouted, 'Surprise!' Scared the *shit* out of Dad. Got whipped for *that* too."

The brothers shared a rare laugh together. Victor forgot for a second that he didn't like his brother.

"That is some funny shit, V, but you know what? I know we are not here to reminisce about old times. This might be a family reunion to you, but there's no food, and I'm not enjoying the company. I have things to *see* and people to *do*. Talk to me. What's your plan?" Victor asked while leaning forward in his chair.

"Don't you mean things to *do* and people to . . . ? Never mind. Of *course*, you don't. Anyway, if you could call *anyone* who would stop or prolong my date of execution, who might that be?"

V's plan was in full force, and it was time to reel in this big fish.

"Why do you ask?"

"Just curious, that's all. I'd like to know who to personally thank just in case they strap me to the chair."

"Well, it would probably be Judge Campbell or the governor. If I call either of them, they will hold off until I call them back and say 'do it.'"

V continued. "Okay, I know you wouldn't represent me in court, that's *obvious* by you not offering to do so, but if there were someone from your office that you would *recommend*, who would *that* be?"

"You sure are asking a lot of invasive ass questions. How is this shit helping you get out of here?"

"Hell, lawyer, I thought *I* was *supposed* to ask the questions. I would think that *you* had all the answers."

"*Fuck* you, V! Your ass is lucky I came! *Bastard!* Okay. Well, let's see. I'm thinking . . . hmm . . . uh, maybe a guy named Chase Morton. He's pretty good."

"Cool. So did you bring that paperwork for me to sign? You know . . . the ones about me leaving the country?"

"Yes, sir, I have them. *That's* a question I was *hoping* you'd ask. Let's get *that* part over with." At this point, Victor started to get happy.

He pulled out the papers and a pen and handed them to V. He pointed out that *if* he were to ever get out of jail and his name was cleared of *all* charges, the person *known* to everyone as V or Vinny or Vincent, were to leave the country. All flights, housing, and any other provision would be made by the Taylor Law Firm. V glanced over the paperwork and then signed the three sheets where his signature was required. Victor took the papers, looked at the signature lines, and then filed them back in his folder. He was smiling by now.

There is one thing about time. It waits for no man and never stops. V knew that some time had elapsed since the beginning of this meeting, but he didn't know exactly how much. It was now time for the dramatic finish. He stared down at the floor.

"Yo, Vic, what time is it?"

"It's eleven twenty-five, and I'm bored."

"You got a cigarette?"

"Yeah. I thought you *quit*. When did *you* start back smoking? Since *this* place? Damn, man, you know cigarettes are no good for you. *Wow.* Would you listen to me? Talking to you like I was your big *brother* or like I *care* or some shit like that."

"Well, you are the older of us two. From what I was told, you beat me by what . . . five minutes? But you know what? You *do* sound sort of stupid telling me *I* shouldn't smoke and *you* still smoke."

V lit his cigarette. Victor did the same.

"Are you calling me *stupid*?"

Victor was a grown man, but he had a lot of childhood issues. He couldn't *stand* to be called anything but positive. He never did learn that sticks and stones could break ones bones, but names could never hurt him.

"No, man, I'm not calling you *anything*! You *know* what I mean."

"Well, you better *not* be because I will walk my ass out of here, and it'll be the *last* thing you see of me! You won't even be able to *kiss* it! Now is there *anything else* you need to discuss with me? I need to get on living my life, and I sure don't *plan* on living it in here!"

Victor was aggravated and impatient at this point.

"Aw-ight, man. I'm sorry. But you do know that plans can change," V said.

"What the fuck does *that* mean?" Victor asked.

V stood up from the table and walked over to the wall furthest from the door with his back to Victor. If V knew his brother like he thought he did, Victor would not be looked down upon. In other words, if V was standing, then Victor could not be seated. He would feel like V was in control, and there was no way he would let that happen. Victor stood up as V anticipated. V became silent. He knew there was only about twenty-five minutes left, and his timing had to be perfect.

"Well? Are we *through*?" Victor asked.

V turned from the wall to face Victor, only to find him close enough for him to hug.

"Not yet. I do have one more question. I need you to be *completely* honest with me. When you decided to come see me today, had you already made up in your mind that no matter *what* I did or said, you would *not* help me?"

Victor looked away because even though he didn't like his brother, he felt a sense of guilt. That didn't happen much. He knew V had him pegged. He looked back at V right dead in his eyes.

"Yes. I had already decided. Except for having you sign that paperwork, which is *my* insurance *if* you get out, you are out of my life for good, I didn't plan on doing a damn thing for you. You deserve every fucking thing you get. I will come back one *more* time, however . . . when they strap your black ass to the electric chair!"

"That's what I thought," V said sadly.

One move. One blow. That's all it took. V had head-butted Victor, gagged him, and had him in the sleeper hold, all in expertly timed actions.

"Sorry, my brother," V whispered in Victor's ear. "You've done all that *you* had to do. This is something that *I* have to do."

Victor was out like a light. He made the mistake of getting too close in the first place. He tried to struggle at first, but it just made him weaker *sooner*. V went to work removing the clothes that he was wearing and then the clothes that Victor had on. The "big switch" was on. He moved as swiftly as possible because he knew that time was *not* on his side. He switched *everything, even* the underwear. He couldn't take *any* chances. Victor's watch was the last thing V removed, and then he placed it on his own wrist. He looked at "his" watch, and it read 11:55 a.m. Perfect! He reached in the inside pocket of the blazer and grabbed the atomizer for a refresher. Then he called out to Kevin.

"Guard! Guard, help!"

Kevin rushed in, saw "Vincent" unconscious, and called on his walkie-talkie for backup.

"What happened?" Kevin inquired.

"Well, at *first*, he was asking a lot of questions and shit, and then he wanted to sample some of my cologne, so I handed him my atomizer. When he handed it back, he tried to jump me. I guess he was going to try to switch places with me or some shit like that! He might know some Bruce Lee shit, but he forgot *I'm* still the older brother, and he doesn't know *what* I know!"

By stating the fact of what had just *occurred* as some sort of hypothetical situation, V threw the dogs off his scent. He had portrayed Victor so many times in the past he knew *exactly* how to sound and act with all the arrogance Victor exuded. This time the *fox* wins.

"Well, this doesn't look too good for V. He's going to have to pay for this kind of behavior. Damn, just got out of solitary too."

"*Really?* Well, Officer . . ." V looked at Kevin's badge as if he didn't know him. "Casey. You know what's *best*, right?"

V could hear the concern in Kevin's voice and began to appreciate him even more. Truth of the matter, if Kevin had not set all this up, the plan would not have been successful, and V actually want to thank him *right then*. As Kevin was picking "Vincent" up off the floor, three other guards appeared on the scene. They took him out, all the while asking if "Atty. Victor Taylor" was all right. He assured them he was fine, but he was ready to leave. Just as he reached the door of the padded cell, one of the guards stopped him.

"Hold on one minute, Mr. Taylor." *Uh oh!* V froze. What on earth did he forget?

"Are *these* your papers here on this table?"

"Yes. Yes, by all means let me grab those. I can't *believe* I almost forgot them. Very important documents, you know. Thank you, sir."

They called for someone to come, and the guard escorted V all the way out to the parking lot and then left him to reach his vehicle. V jingled the keys that were in his pocket. He didn't have the slightest idea what Victor was driving these days. He looked at the key ring and noticed the Maybach logo. Whatever it was, it was nice. He took a breath of fresh air and pushed the alarm on the keys. The vehicle that flashed had a license plate on it that read, MYWRLD. A 2015 light blue/dark brown Maybach. *Should have known,* thought V. He couldn't really believe it, but he was *out*. As he punched the alarm system off with the remote, he couldn't help but smile. He got in, started up the vehicle, and was greeted to the sounds of Marvin Gaye's "Trouble Man." He rubbed his forehead.

"Damn head as hard as a *brick*!"

As he drove up to the gate to leave, he put the shades on that Victor had put in his pocket. He rolled down the window to be face-to-face with his true test. Officer Jebediah Cooper was back at the gate entrance/exit.

"Well, Mr. Taylor, I hope you saw for *yourself* that your brother has been *well* taken care of, right?" Cooper asked with his possum grin. He had a little less piss than before.

"*Actually*, my brother told me about one of the guards here giving him a crappy time. As a matter of fact, it was *you* that he mentioned."

V removed the shades and stared Cooper right in his eyes with sternness.

Pass this test, V! Pass this test!

"Well, I, uh . . . I . . . well," Cooper sputtered.

"Well, my *ass*! Look, I know that you are going to do *some* things to the inmates. It's probably in your nature. And I also get the feeling you don't like Vincent all that much. I'm *right*, aren't I? I don't like him much, either, but if he's going to get fucked over, it'll be by *me* from now on. All I'm saying is ease up a little on my brother. Understand?"

"Yes, sir, Mr. Taylor. You won't have to mention it again."

"Good. Make doubly sure of it, or you're going to have a well-whipped ass!"

V put the shades back on and sped from the gate, headed for the freeway. He knew that if this had been a *real* class, in a *real* school, taking a *real* test, he would have earned an A+.

CHAPTER 15

REALITY SHOW

"Well, I'll just be *damned*! I can't *believe* what just happened!" V said, referring to his plan. It had worked through to perfection, and he had to try to find a *new* focus. The CD playing in the radio switched to Marvin Gaye's "What's Going On?" It was good to hear *regular* music again instead of made-up stuff by the inmates. Somebody rapping, somebody else thinking they sounded like Luther Vandross when they really sounded like Bob Dylan, and then there was someone else singing a gospel hymn. At least the gospel singer could carry a tune, but there was nothing like hearing some Marvin in a big roomy vehicle with that new car smell. And there was nothing like *not* being in prison. V's new focus had to be on how to prove his innocence for someone's murder.

Can't forget to call those people Victor told me about. If I don't, a particular prisoner will die, V thought. *I'm just glad that Victor "graciously accepted" to change places with me. Well, hell, you know. I do know this: Junior would be proud of me right now and probably jealous because he didn't have anything to do with it!*

V did all this thinking while driving straight to the cemetery. He didn't even realize that he was even going there until he reached the entrance to it. Once there, however, he knew why. He was there to visit his father's grave. It had been over three years since the last time he went there. He stopped the vehicle on the road a few yards from the tombstone, got out, and walked up to it. He brushed off the leaves that had halfway covered the spot. The tombstone read, "Thomas Taylor, a fine man, surely missed, always loved. Jan. 10, 1949–Feb. 18, 2007." V looked down and spoke to the man known as his father.

"Well. It's been a while, huh? I don't really know what made me come to visit, but I did *think* about you while I was in prison. I miss you a lot. How do I *look*? I really believe had you still been alive, I wouldn't have gotten into the trouble that I have. Besides, you would have whipped my ass the *first* time I went in, and I'm sure that would have been the last time I would give you or Moms any grief. Lately, it seems like I have a lot of apologizing to do to a whole lot of people: you, Moms, Cassandra, and when I figure all this out, even Victor. By the way, he says hi. Okay, you know I'm lying. I wish you were here to help me. I'm positive that if you were here, you would *already* know what to do. Anyway, if you went to heaven, put in a good word for me. I can use all the help I can get. If you didn't go to heaven, don't say shit. I've already done my share of hell right here on earth, and the last thing I need is for someone to put in a good word for me to go to hell. Actually, I don't even want to think about it. My mind says you went up. I'll always have a place for you in my heart. I love you, and I'll come back to see you again. *Sooner* this time. I promise."

The Samsung G7 that was in Victor's blazer pocket rang out with the music of Beethoven's "Ninth Symphony," and V answered it in classic Victor Taylor fashion.

"Victor Taylor. It's your dime, but it's my time."

"Hey, baby!"

Baby? Oh shit! Terri! I forgot about Victor's wife!

"Terri? Oh hi. What's up?"

"What's *up*? Why did you answer your phone that way with *me*? Didn't you look at the screen to see who was calling?"

V was in such a hurry to act like Victor he didn't even think.

"I'm sorry, bae. Got caught up with this V shit. I didn't even think."

"Oh okay. I was just calling to see where you were and if you still wanted to go out to dinner tonight."

V swallowed. "Dinner? Yeah, sure. Do you want *me* to make the plans or what?"

"You told *me* to make the plans, remember?"

V didn't remember because V wasn't Victor. He didn't know anything. He would have to be more careful in the future.

"Oh yeah, I remember now. Is everything set?"

"Just about. How *did* your meeting go?"

If Terri could see the smile that broke out on V's face, she would have known something was up. But since she couldn't . . .

"My *meeting*? My meeting is *probably* the reason why I'm not remembering all that well. You see, that asshole attacked me, and my head is *still* hurting."

V now had the perfect excuse for saying, thinking, or doing *anything* out of the ordinary.

"*Attacked?* What do you mean, *attacked?* Vic, what *happened?* Where *are* you? You probably need to come home and lie down for a while. *Maybe* even see a doctor! You know we could *postpone* this dinner if you'd like. Are you telling me that V *attacked* you?"

"Calm down, Terri, I'm fine. Just a head butt, that's all. I just don't remember all that well, okay? I'll be all right. I've got a few errands to run, but I'll be home later, aw-ight? Ahem . . . *all right?*"

"Okay. The reservations have been made for eight o'clock, but I've still got some beautifying to do to myself. Is that time good for you?"

"Yeah, Terri, that's perfect. I'll try to be home about six, okay?"

"Okay. See you then. Love you."

"Yeah, uh . . . love you too."

V hung up and put the phone on his forehead, knowing well that he wasn't prepared for that. V had portrayed Victor on numerous occasions, but there was one portrayal he had never taken on before: being a husband. He didn't know if Victor even *told* Terri he loved her. He didn't know if they hugged or kissed. Were they playful or nasty to each other? He was in the dark. This made things a bit sticky for V. Dinner in the past with anyone *he* would take out most times led to bigger and better things later in the evening. Something told him this evening would *not* be any different.

"Well, well," V said to himself, "this is going to be quite an interesting evening. And it looks to be rewarding as well!"

But what about Cassie? he thought. *She's just going to have to wait until this is over.*

V would not let anything or *anyone* blow his cover. Not Cassie, Terri, Moms, and since Victor was "standing in" for V, *especially* not him.

"There's one thing I'm *damn* sure of: I have *got* to change this *ring tone!*"

* * *

Riinngg!

"Hello?"

"*Hey*, Moms! How are you *doing*?"

"Moms? Moms who?"

"Moms Taylor. Mrs. *Elaine* Taylor."

"Who is this?"

"This is Junior."

"Junior? Junior *who*?"

"Junior *Martin*! You know, *Vincent's* friend."

"Vincent? Vincent who?"

"Moms? This *is* you, right? Are you okay?"

Moms was biting her tongue trying to keep from laughing over the phone. She held out as long as she could and let out a big guffaw in the phone speaker.

"Wow! Moms, you had me *worried* there for a minute. Seriously, though, are you all right?" Junior asked with concern.

"Yeah, baby, I'm *fine*. I had you *going* there, didn't I?"

"Sure the hell did! Excuse my French. Anyway, I'm in town at Aunt Jen's. Got home a little faster than I thought. I think I'll go see V tomorrow, but I'm *beat* now. All that driving. They allow visitors on Sundays, don't they?"

"I think so, but if I were you, I'd call first. But even if they don't allow visitors, guess what?"

"What?"

"I'm cooking tomorrow, and you're invited. Wanna come?"

"Do I want to come? You'd better believe it! Oh, by the way, can I bring a friend?"

"A *friend*, huh? Is this a boyfriend? Are you gay?"

"Nope. Not gay. This is a *girl* friend. Wow!"

"Don't get me wrong, Junior. I wouldn't mind it if you *were* gay. Now if you don't want to tell me . . ."

"Well, I'm not *gay*, damnit! Sorry about that, Moms, but you're messing with my mind. Seriously? Would that be a problem for you if I *was*?"

Moms just laughed at her poking fun at Junior. She didn't really figure that he *was* gay, but he was like one of her own sons, so it really wouldn't matter if he were. She hadn't talked to her other "son" in a while, and she was just being playful.

"No, son, it wouldn't be a problem for me. But I see it's a problem for *you*. Sooo," Moms said, "this friend of yours is a *female*, right?"

"Yes, ma'am, my friend is female, and I *believe* you will love her. Like *I* do," he said almost uncontrollably. Patricia was looking and listening to the entire conversation on speakerphone anyway, and this brought a big smile to her face. She blew a kiss at him and whispered the words "olive juice." Junior thought she said "I love you." Even though *this* time she didn't say the words, she really did love him too, and Junior was hooked.

"*Love?* Are you growing up, Mr. Martin? Never mind, don't answer that. Are you getting married? Wait. Don't answer that either. Is she pregnant? Hell, don't answer *that* one either. It's hard enough to think about my boys growing up on me. For one thing, it makes me feel old. *Please* bring your friend. You know I wouldn't have it any other way."

"Thanks, Moms! What time is dinner going to be served?"

"Everything ought to be done by one. But if you're *late*, you'll miss your *plate*. For you *and* your *date*, I will not *wait*. We'll *celebrate*, but we'll lock the *gate*. And your *fate*, you'll *hate* because of the food *we ate*."

Junior and Patricia were both laughing by now.

"Moms, you're crazy. But I have some advice for you: Leave the rapping to the professionals."

"What? You trying to *hate*? Boy, you better *appreciate*! Rapping's my new *trait*!"

"Well, I hope it's not your new *job*. You're a *slob*!"

"Oooo, that was low, and you'll pay for that, Mr. Junior! I still love you though."

"Love you too, Moms. We'll see you tomorrow. And we won't *procrastinate* or be late."

They hung up, and Junior grabbed a quilt out of the linen closet and headed for the couch in the living room. He and Patricia had been on the road for quite a while, and 1,300 miles can catch up to you. Pat had hinted for the past two days about getting together on a sexual tone, but as bad as Junior wanted to break a back, he would not disrespect his aunt or uncle. Aunt Jenny showed Patricia the upstairs bedroom that Junior usually slept in when he was there, but she didn't have to say a word to him about sleeping on the couch. He knew. But at least he was finally home; he had a woman who *claimed* she loved him for him, a few new rags, a new career, and a pocketful of money. He wasn't rich, but he certainly wasn't poor either. He was exhausted though. He and Patricia deserved to spend some quality time together, but for tonight, respect and sleep were the order of the day.

"Patience is a virtue," Moms would always say.

Just as Junior nodded off to sleep, Patricia kissed him on the forehead before heading upstairs. She thought, *There just has to be some hotel vacancies somewhere in this city. Junior should already know this, but, Google, don't let me down!*

CHAPTER 16

UNKNOWN TERRI-TORY

"Daammnn!"
V was driving up to the "Taylor Estate," as his brother always called it. Forty acres of perfectly landscaped grounds with a few trees placed strategically on the lawn. A half of a mile driveway, security gate, and fenced in. Ten-thousand-square-foot brick and marble home. Just driving up to the front gate was quite impressive. As V drove up to the gate, there was a motion-activated voice box, along with a video camera. This would prove to be a challenge for V, seeing as how the gate would automatically open for Terri's and Victor's voices. There was a sensor that detected if the vehicles pulling up belonged to them or to a stranger. The sensor recognized the Maybach and "Victor Taylor."

"*Hello, Mr. Taylor. Please make your request,*" the box spoke in its computerized voice. V didn't count on *all* the tests involved with his freedom, but then again, he wasn't *truly* free.

"*Open* sez a me," he said in his best Victor impression.

There was a small pause and then a whirring sound as the gate opened to allow passage through. It didn't matter *what* was said as long as the computer recognized the voice of "Victor." As V drove up the long winding driveway, he couldn't help but be impressed. He couldn't figure out how his brother found such a location on the outskirts of New York. How his brother didn't appreciate what he had. How grass stayed green year-round even through the snow and ice. Victor could *have* just about anything money could buy, including people, but most times he just used them for his advantage. They, along with his possessions, were just conquests to brag about.

As V reached the house, he pushed the garage door opener to the four-car garage. As it opened, it revealed the only spot available to park. The others were already occupied. A red Jaguar XJ6. A silver Mercedes Benz CLZ. A black Ferrari. All clean, all less than a year old.

"Daammnn!" V said. He was truly in awe of his surroundings. But then, even though it was just land, a house, and vehicles, who wouldn't be to some sort of degree?

"Boy, I can't wait to drive that Ferrari! Shit, that's a *bad* motherfucker right there!"

As he closed the garage door, he looked in the vehicles and saw some tissue in the front seat and a tennis racket on the floor of the Jag. He figured this to be Terri's car. Well-needed information.

"Terri? I'm home," he called out as he entered he door connecting the garage to the house. He walked through the kitchen that sparkled like new quarters with marble floors, cabinets galore, and the largest refrigerator V had ever seen. He continued on until he reached the den, where a fire was blazing in the fireplace. He knew his way around the house pretty well, seeing as how he helped his brother and sister-in-law move in after they finished building it. Knowing how much Victor detested Vincent, it surprised V that his brother would allow him to help with the moving. It was free labor, and that *had* to explain it all. The house was immaculate. V walked out of the den to the stairs where he *had* to stop. At the top of the stairs stood Terri. She had on a dress that revealed one of Terri's more beautiful assets. It was a pretty royal blue that fit like a corset at the top and had a long slit up one side of it. Her hair was pulled up, and she wore a lovely string of pearls. She looked like one of the actresses you see on Oscar night. With her Caribbean looks and her toned body, Terri was the envy of a lot of women and men too. Women wished they could *look* like her, and men wished that they could *be* with her. V had seen a few women since he left prison on his drive in, but none of them had gotten the "treatment" Terri had gotten that day, and none of them looked as beautiful as the creature that stood before him. Even now, *he* envied his *brother*, not for his *material* possessions, but for the true treasure that his eyes beheld.

"Hey, *baby*. You *like* what you see?" Terri asked seductively. V could only nod. She was gorgeous.

"Well, don't just *stand* there with your mouth wide-open. Come and give me a kiss," she beckoned.

V walked up the stairs kind of quickly, almost tripping. He played it off, though, as if he did it on purpose. When he reached the top, he held Terri close and gave her a long tongue-swapping kiss. He didn't really want to, but at the same time, he sorta did. He sure wasn't objecting to it. He really didn't know what might have gone down between Terri and Victor this day, this week, this year even, so he had to *always* play everything by ear. He didn't realize that Terri was such a fantastic kisser though. That was a nice surprise. He felt *he* was, but he knew *nothing* about this woman. Her lips were *amazing*. It was only after coming up for air did he realize how long the kiss really was. It was a good thing he used those Listerine strips right before he came in. That was a tip from Junior: Never offend in the breath department.

"Damn, baby! You must be feeling a *lot* better! Where did you get hit?" Terri inquired.

V had *almost* forgotten his story.

"Huh? Oh, it was right here on my forehead. Can you believe him *head-butting me*? I guess he didn't figure how hard *my* head was. Oh, and by the way . . . this is for you." V handed her a single rose. "Happy Valentine's Day, baby."

"Oh, *thank* you, Victor! How *sweet*! I wasn't going to say anything, but I thought you'd forgotten . . . like *last* year. Anyway, about your hard *head*? Hell, *yeah*! *Everyone* should *already* know that. Ha ha! Here, let me kiss it for you."

While Terri paid attention to the "boo boo" on V's head, he thought to himself, *Damn, Terri's a tender, loving, caring woman, and some TLC is just what I need. I'm afraid I could get used to this! I wonder if Victor would agree to us staying like this* even *when he gets out . . . that is,* if *he gets out. Hell, he's got to get out! He's me!*

"You know, baby, you're right on time. But then again, I didn't really expect you to be late. I ran you a hot bath. I would join you, but then we might not *ever* go out to dinner, and you wouldn't be able to make it up to me like you said you would. Besides, we have all evening, right?"

V almost said that it would be okay to join him, but after finding out that his brother had to atone for "whatever," he thought differently. Play it by ear.

"Yeah, we wouldn't want to spoil my plans now, would we?" V asked. "You made all the eating arrangements, right?"

"Sure did," she answered. "You like Jacques', right?"

"Hell yeah!" V said. He really didn't have a clue about Jacques', unless it was a fancy way of saying jack-in-the-box, but he didn't believe that. Jacques' sounded pricy, but he had to remind himself of who he was portraying and who was *really* paying for the meal. The fantabulous Victor Taylor. Everyone knows *he* got it. *Thanks, bro!*

"And after dinner, I have *other* surprises for you, okay?" V said.

"Okay. What? Are you bringing your 'A' game?" Terri said with a question-mark look on her face. She liked this "mystery man" in front of her. It was a different spin from what she was used to, and it made her feel all tingly. Although V would have to make up these "surprise plans" along the way, he felt more confident he was saying the right things. He didn't answer. He just headed to the bathroom and started to undress to get in his bath.

"Oh, I almost forgot," Terri called out, "Moms called and wanted to confirm us for dinner tomorrow. I told her we'd be there. Was I right?"

Hell yeah!

"Oh yeah, you were *so* right!"

V finally got to "his" underwear, took them off, and then slipped down into the hot and soothing tub of water. It was big enough for three people to fit in comfortably. If one didn't know better, one would think that Victor *planned* it that way. V saw a button on the side of the tub and pushed it. The water started churning and spinning all around him.

Hells yeah! This feels damn good! Wait a minute! Terri said Moms called. He hadn't even tried to contact Moms after he got out. It was probably for the better though. He might have tipped his hand, and it was *much* too early in the game to be doing that.

"Hey, Terri! Should we take your car tonight?" he yelled out.

She called back on the intercom next to the Jacuzzi. "Why are you yelling? Did you forget about the intercom system you had installed?"

Shit!

V pushed the talk button. "Sorry, babe. I *did* forget. Can you *ever* forgive me?"

What? Victor apologizing? And in a playful way? What the hell? Terri thought.

"Yeah, sweetie, I can forgive you. Now what were you trying to ask me?"

"Oh. Should we take *your* car tonight, or what?"

He usually makes that decision. He must have been hit hard!

"Uh, how about we take the Mercedes?"

"Okay. I'll see you in a few."

That helped matters even more for V. He knew that the Ferrari and the Maybach were Victor's, so as far as V was concerned, the vehicle situation was clear.

He got out of the tub, toweled himself dry, and then wrapped the towel around him as he went into the bedroom. It felt *real* good to take a normal bath alone instead of a shower with a bunch of men. After seeing what Terri had on, he hoped that whatever he chose to wear would complement her.

He found a nice Italian dark blue suit, white pinstripe shirt, and a blue and pink printed silk tie. The fabric of the shirt alone felt like nothing he'd ever felt, but once he put it on, he *knew* he looked good. He found some blue socks, not too flashy because he didn't want to take attention away from the suit, and some brown Steve Madden shoes. He was ready . . . for what though? He would just have to find out.

He came down the stairs to find Terri in the den with a glass of "something" in her hand. Her legs were crossed, and they came through the slit of the dress. Fine was an understatement for what Terri was, and what V saw caused a rise in his pants. The suit did give him some leeway so that even though it was unnoticeable, it was uncomfortable and uncontrollable.

"You want one?" Terri asked, holding up her glass.

"Naw, I better not. I'm driving."

"Hmmm, smart *and* sensible. So are you ready to go?"

"Yeah, *you*?"

"I'm as ready as I'll *ever* be. I'm really looking forward to this evening. I just hope that *you* are! By the way, you look *very* nice! Very *well-groomed*! Very *sexy*!"

"Thank you, but not near as nice as you, Ms. Lady. You've got to be the finest woman on this planet!" V was viewing Terri in a different light tonight.

"Why, thank you, sir, but if I *am* fine, it's only because I'm with the finest *man* in the world!"

"That's laying it on a little *thick*, but . . . okay, if you *say* so."

They both laughed as they headed out the door toward the garage. He held her hand as he escorted her to their car. If a lady ever wants to boost her man's ego and make him feel he is the most important person in her life, saying that he looks very good or that he is the finest man in the world doesn't hurt. The only problem in this case is that V realized and understood that he was not *really* Terri's man. He had to focus on this evening and, after tonight, one day at a time. If it meant staying away from Cassie, perpetrating his brother, deceiving his best friend, sexing his sister-in-law, or avoiding eye contact with his mother, he would do it all and more to clear his name.

CHAPTER 17

SUNDAY'S BEST

It was about one thirty in the afternoon, but Moms had left church a little bit earlier than she usually did to make sure all would be done when her family and guests arrived for dinner. She had an apron tied around her waist and was busy putting the frosting on a devil's food cake. She thought for a minute why someone would name anything after the devil, especially if it tasted as good as this. She could understand naming an angel's food cake or a better-than-sex cake, but the devil should get no credit for what she just created. She had been told before, however, that it should be a sin for anything to be as good as her cooking. It tickled her to think about a better-than-sex cake.

That ain't ever gonna be true, she thought, smiling.

Her doorbell rang, and she went to greet her first arrival.

"Pastor Stanley! Wow! Did you even *do* the benediction? Come on in. I don't even have to ask if you're *hungry*, do I?"

It figured that the *preacher* would be the first one to arrive.

"Yes, ma'am, Sister Taylor, I *am* hungry! You know us preacher folk loves to eat. It smells heavenly too! Is that *chicken* I smell?"

"You wish, don't you? Fried pork chops. I also made some, some macaroni and cheese, some sweet potato casserole, some fried okra, and I'll cook some hot water cornbread when the majority of the people get here. Oh, and, Pastor?"

"Yeah?"

"I made some fried chicken too. I knew you'd appreciate that."

"Hoo, thank you, sister! You know I love that yard bird. What's for dessert?"

"Devil's food cake, peach cobbler, and banana pudding."

"Hoo, lawd, *all* that sounds sinful! You make sure I get a double portion, you hear?"

"Ooo, Pastor, you ought to be ashamed!"

They both laughed.

"Here, let me take your coat and your hat and you go on in the den. You can cut the TV on. I'll let you know when everything's done."

As the pastor headed toward the den and before Moms could close the front door, she saw Junior drive up with his friend. Instead of closing the door, she just stood there and waited for them to make it to where she was. She looked at Patricia and thought to herself, *Cute. But cute ain't everything.*

"Moms! It's so good to see you!" Junior said while giving Moms a big hug and kiss on the cheek. "Moms. Allow me to introduce to you, Patricia C. Jackson. Patricia, this is Moms."

"I've heard so much about you, Ms. Taylor! It's a pleasure to meet you!" Patricia said oh so politely. Moms saw in this girl's eyes a genuine honesty not seen in a lot of people nowadays. This would go a long way.

"The pleasure is all mine, sugar. Come on in and make yourselves at home. By the way, what's the 'C' stand for?"

"Do you mean in her name? She won't even tell *me* and she's supposed to *love* me," Junior said.

"Oh well, don't worry about it then. It's a good thing you guys are not late, or did Junior not tell you the consequences?"

"Yes, ma'am, I heard. I think he took you to be *serious*."

"Honey, Junior *knows* me. I *was* serious! Now what's the 'C' stand for?"

"Well, it stands for the first initial of my daddy's last name. I've been with my mother for so long it was confusing using his last name when she went back to her maiden name after they split. It's just paying homage to him without upsetting my mother. Back home, it stopped people from asking so many questions."

"Oh. Is he still alive?" Moms gave Patricia a serious look that took Pat by surprise. She didn't expect for Moms to be a callous person, especially after the way Junior bragged on her. As Moms headed for the kitchen, she looked over her shoulder and gave Pat a wink. This eased Pat's mind and let her know that Moms was only playing and everything was as she hoped.

"In my heart, I believe he is, but I'm not really sure. My mother won't say. Could you use some help in there, Ms. Taylor?" Pat asked.

"Not really, but I will accept the company. Besides, I'd like to get to know you better. You game?"

"Sure, I'm not afraid."

"Maybe you *should* be. Junior, could you get the door for me?"

"Sure, Moms . . . Good luck," he said to Pat, winking at her.

No sooner than they exited, the doorbell rang again. Junior hung up his and Pat's coats and then went to the door, only to find standing in front of him Terri and who he thought was Victor Taylor. V was so glad to see his best friend he almost risked everything just to embrace him. He knew he had to play it cool though.

"Hi, Terri! It's good to see you! You too, Victor . . . I guess. Come on in. Moms is in the kitchen with my fian . . . er, my friend."

"Your *what*? I *heard* you. You were about to say *fiancée*, weren't you? Are you getting married, Junior? When did you get in?" Terri asked.

"No, in reality, I haven't asked her to marry me yet. Got in yesterday. I came home to see if there was anything I could do to help V. Unlike *some* people," he said while glancing at "Victor."

"Hey, look, for *your* information, I went to the prison yesterday to listen to some cockamamie plan of his, only to be *attacked* by that bastard! Have *you* visited him since *you* got here?" V said.

"I tried to today, but they told me he was on lockdown for at least three weeks! They also told me he got beat up pretty bad. Did all this happen because he attacked you? Yeah, they told me *that* too."

"Probably." V hadn't heard anything since he got out. He was only concerned with getting out, but he didn't consider what might happen to his brother after the switch. He sort of anticipated the extra time in the hole but not the beating.

"Look, I'm sorry for your friend, but he's most likely getting everything he deserves."

"*Fuck* you, Victor! He may be my friend, but he's *your* brother, and you treat him like he *stole* from you or something!"

"Look, don't get your ass kicked up in here! I'll tell you what you can do. You can kiss—"

"*Victor!* I *thought* I heard your voice. I'm so glad you decided to come! Hey, Terri! Girl, you are glowing!" Moms's interruption saved a whole lot of trouble. Had she not entered the room when she did, V would have been moving furniture with his best friend in the world. He probably would've hurt him, but he really didn't know what Junior knew. Could've gotten hurt himself, come to think of it.

Moms was hugging everyone by now. She was just happy to have her family and friends over for dinner, but she felt a little bad that one of her sons could not be there with her. While she thought about her other child, the doorbell rang again, and it almost scared her. She went to the door and opened it.

"Hey, Moms! How are you doing?"

Cassandra! What the hell? V thought.

"Hey, Junior! When did you get in?"

"Yesterday," Moms answered for him like he was her other son.

"Well, you sure are looking *good*! Hi, Terri . . . Victor. You guys all right?"

Terri grabbed V around the waist.

"We're *fine*, thank you. And you?"

"*Busy*, girlfriend. You know, I've got a new modeling job. It's hard when you're not five feet ten inches and skinny. I got some booty though . . . Oh, I guess you can already see that, huh?" Cassie said while turning to expose her backside, especially for the guys.

"Yeah . . . we *noticed*," Terri responded. She was trying to be nice, but she knew Cassandra was a bit flirty. She held on to "Victor" even tighter.

"Who's your friend?" Moms asked, referring to the gentleman standing behind Cassie.

Yeah! Who's your damn friend? thought V. He wanted so badly to voice this out loud.

"Oh . . . everyone, this is Roger. And don't worry, Moms, he is *only* a friend. He's one of the photographers working on our shoot. I told him you were cooking, and he wanted to come. Is it okay?"

No! thought V.

"Sure! There's plenty. Come on in," Moms said.

"Okay. Roger, this is Moms, Junior, Terri, and the famous Victor Taylor!"

"*You're* Victor Taylor? The *real* Victor Taylor? Wow, your reputation precedes you! I was wondering if you have some time, I'd like to talk about a legal matter I'm dealing with," Roger said.

"You can have one of my cards and call my office. I don't like to mix business with pleasure, and when Moms *cooks*, it's *nothing* but pure pleasure. Understand?"

"Yes, sir, Mr. Taylor, I *fully* understand. Expect my call though."

"Right."

V knew better than to try to talk shop when it would be obvious to everyone he didn't know *what* he would be talking about. He just had to make it through one day at a time.

"Well, let's go sit at the table. Everything's done," Moms suggested.

As they headed for the dining room, Moms went into the den, where she had to wake up Pastor Stanley. When they entered, she noticed that Patricia had practically set all the food and the place settings on the table. This brought a big grin to Moms's face. As they all were seated, Moms asked the pastor to say the blessings on the food.

"Just try not to be *long-winded*, okay?" V said in his best Victor Taylor impression.

The preacher began, "Lord, we thank you for the people that you have allowed to assemble here today. Some from afar and some from nearby. Bless the hands that have prepared this food. Bless us that we may partake of this food and that it might be nourishing to our bodies that we may use it to be of service to you. Bless this food so that—"

"Amen!" interrupted V. "*Damn*, preacher! Long-winded in the pulpit *and* at the dinner table!"

"*Victor*! Your manners, son!"

"Okay, okay, but I *told* him not to be long-winded. Hell, if I had wanted to hear a sermon *and* take a nap, I would have gone to *church*!"

This was classic Victor Taylor, and V was quite proud to have pulled it off.

CHAPTER 18

INSERT FOOT

Victor woke up on Sunday morning, looked up, and rose from the cot he was lying on. It was dark in the room he now occupied, and it smelled of piss. He grabbed his head with both hands; although he had a killer headache, he also noticed the aches and pains in other parts of his body. He touched the fabric of the cloth that surrounded his body, and he knew right away it wasn't the same clothes he had put on that morning. Those clothes were soft to the touch and finely pressed; these clothes had a cotton roughness about them and an odor of clothes washed in cheap detergent mixed with day-old funk. He didn't know it, but he was the "special guest" in the "special room." He was trying to recollect his thoughts, but everything was fuzzy.

"Well, you fucked up *real* good this time, *didn't* you Vinshit?" Cooper called to Victor from outside the cell door.

Vinshit? Is he referring to V? Where am I? Who the hell is this person anyway?

Victor had always played dirty and *always* tipped the scales in his favor. He'd pretty much sold his soul to the devil, but he didn't figure he would spend his time in hell still on earth. At the present, what he was certain of was the pain he was experiencing. It all started to come back to him; he had a meeting with V.

He wouldn't *switch places with me, would he? Did he? Aw shit,* of course, *he would, and I'll just be* damned *if he didn't!*

"Excuse me . . . *Officer*? There has been a *terrible* misunderstanding which has led to a *horrible* mistake. *Excuse* me? Do you *hear* me?" Victor called out to Cooper.

"Yeah, *I* hear you, but the only misunderstanding here is that my *friends* didn't realize they should have *killed* your ass! I just *hate* <u>I</u> wasn't there," Cooper said.

"Look, sir, my head hurts, and my thoughts are cloudy. What did I do to deserve a *beat-down*?" Victor asked, trying to receive as much information as he could.

"Sir? Shit, they *did* knock you *senseless*, huh? I was thinking since you weren't *dead*, maybe they knocked some sense *into* that thick skull of yours. You *really* don't remember?"

"No. I don't."

"Well, let's see now. You had a meeting with your attorney brother, and during the meeting, you tried to attack him. I guess you thought you could trade places or some shit like that. When my boys got to you, they tell me your brother was *very* agitated and had to show you *exactly* who *he* was. He kicked your *ass*, actually knocked you the fuck *out!*"

Cooper told this story as if he were telling a bedtime story to a two-year-old. He did wish he had been there, but if he had, he wouldn't be *having* this conversation with who he *thought* was Vincent. Although it really was Victor, it wouldn't have mattered. He would have been a dead Taylor son either way.

Victor couldn't even respond to what he was just told. He already knew, hoping it was just a dream. It wasn't though. The pain was too real. He just leaned his back against the cold wall and wondered, *Was this V's plan all along? Does he plan on letting me take his place in the electric chair? Hell, did he* have *to head-butt me so damn hard?* He now had to figure a way out of this predicament. He knew asking V to revisit him would be out of the question. Being an attorney, he knew that attacking someone while visiting carried a punishment of some sort, but he didn't know how long he would be in this hole.

"How long am I in here for?"

"Not long enough. Just three weeks."

Three weeks*! Damn.*

* * *

V was all smiles as he drove down the road from his mother's house. Terri had leaned the seat back and was rubbing her stomach. Moms threw down. The dinner was good, but V felt better about a couple of other things. No one noticed he *wasn't* who he pretended to be, or at least no one let on, but what was really making him smile right now was the way Moms reacted to Pastor Stanley. V just couldn't help thinking about it.

"You know, Sister Taylor, that was a mighty fine meal! Mighty fine! I think I better stay out of the grocery store right now. Someone might mistake me for a Thanksgiving turkey 'cause Lord knows I'm stuffed!"

"Well, thank you, Pastor," Moms replied, just grinning. She took much pride in her cooking, and it really pleased her someone rather than her own children enjoyed it just as much.

"You're quite welcome. And you even invited the right people over here today. I mean, you could have had *troublemakers* here."

Moms gave him a look that says "What you talking 'bout, Willis?"

"What are you trying to say, Pastor? Are you talking about someone in *particular*?" Moms asked, never taking her eyes off him.

"Well, I was just referring to Vincent. You know, I've been praying for that boy of yours, but let's be honest here, he ain't *ever* going to amount to much. I just think it would have been a travesty to ruin all this good company with his presence. *That's* all I'm saying."

"Oh," Moms said. "Would you excuse me for a moment?" she asked the pastor. He nodded his approval as she left out of the room. He then turned his attention to the target of his comments, V. Of course, he was unaware of that fact.

"You know what I'm saying, don't you, Victor?" the pastor asked, trying to get some support for his statements.

"Oh yes, and I agree wholeheartedly," V responded. It actually hurt his feelings to know that Pastor Stanley felt this way about him. It was V, not Victor, who always helped cut the grass at the church when they were younger. Victor *never* did anything for anyone unless he reaped some type of benefit. As far as Victor was concerned, if you're not paying, then he's not playing.

"Good. I'm glad you can see that I'm not in this conversation all by my..."

Before he could finish his sentence, he heard the cocking sound of a shotgun. Moms was standing there with a 30/30 rifle in her hands, and she looked like she knew how to use it.

"Get *out*! You get the *hell* out of my house! You made your point about my son. Now I'm making *mine* about you!"

"*Sister Taylor!* That's not very Christian-like!" the pastor said while falling out of the chair he sat in. He crawled around behind it, trying to hide.

"Don't be trying to hide, Pastor. This gun can shoot through a tree, so some cushion and some fabric shouldn't hinder this any. I made my confession for Christ a long time ago, and if I'm not mistaken, even *he* kicked some people out of *his* house who were in the wrong! That's my son you *decided* to talk about and in *my* house too! It is *not* your place to pass judgment on *anyone*! *You*, above all people, should know this. But you decided to do it in my house and *about* one of my *children*! Are you *crazy*? You *know* my husband and I never took no *shit*, and just because he's not here no more don't mean I'm gonna start now! Not one of you in this room is going to talk about my Vincent. Not even you, Victor. You do *not* talk about your brother, you *hear* me?"

"Moms, I'm sorry, but I don't care *what* you say. He's *still* a punk to me," V answered, hoping he would be able to get away with this. Classic Victor Taylor statement.

"Okay, Victor. I *know* you. But the *rest* of you might want to think twice about doing it. Oh, and by the way, Pastor, shouldn't your ass be *gone* by now?"

You should have seen how *fast* Pastor Stanley got out of the house of Moms. And the way he was running had the appearance he had an "accident." You can't really blame him. If someone had a shotgun in your face, it would probably produce the same effects as well. First, you'd say it; then you'd do it. *SHIT.*

V spoke up in the typical Victor Taylor manner.

"Good! He finally left. I brought some Hennessy. Anyone game?"

I guess either everyone *else* was glad the pastor left or they just needed a drink because they *all* took a shot. They were *definitely* glad V brought it.

CHAPTER 19

IF YOU DON'T KNOW ME BY NOW . . .

V was pleased his mother felt so strongly about him even if he wasn't a lawyer or a doctor or anything to brag about, for that matter. She loved him because he was hers. It's a good feeling to be loved for who you *are* and *not* what you *do*. He hopes he has this in his relationship with Cassie. But then again, he's not *with* Cassie; he's with *Terri*. Anyway, to V, it was a funny scene with the pastor, and he found himself letting out a laugh.

Terri opened her eyes. "Are you okay?" she asked.

"Yeah. Just thinking about Moms and that shotgun. That was *funny* to *me*! I don't know *why* she made all that fuss about V though. It was *still* some funny shit!"

"Boy, you're *crazy*! Speaking back to your mother when she *told* you no to say anything about V. She could have blown your damn *head* off!" Terri said with concern.

"Nah, *that* wouldn't happen. The way Moms feels about *one* of us, she feels the same about the other. That's what *I* believe anyway."

V didn't just believe; he *knew* this now.

"Besides," he continued, "if I weren't *around*, Moms wouldn't be able to *see* her *other* son, seeing as how we look so much alike."

"Yeah, you two *are* splitting images. If it weren't for your different attitudes and actions, *I* might find it hard to tell you two apart. But *I* can tell the difference. I do like the change in your attitude and demeanor though. And *last night*? Shiiit!" Terri said, settling back down in her seat. Terri was *certain* she knew the differences between Victor and V. Funny how wrong you can be about a person, isn't it?

"What?" V asked. Terri didn't answer. She just closed her eyes and smiled.

The thought that Terri was sure the man driving her home and drove her crazy last night with passionate lovemaking was her very own Victor Taylor made V smile even more. He knew what she meant. He wasn't completely sure he would be able to get away with a bedroom scene with Terri, but she seemed to be more than pleased and never said anything that would deny that fact. He didn't doubt his *own* lovemaking techniques, and Terri *wasn't* his wife, but he knew he had to do whatever was necessary to clear his name. No hesitation. No regrets. It was messed up, he knew that, but his life was on the line . . . and now Victor's as well.

"Say, Terri, I'm going to drop you off at home and then meet up with Junior. He wants to discuss some things with me, so I'm seeing him in town. Is that okay with you?" V asked, trying to catch Terri before she nodded off.

"Yeah, that's fine. I'm tired anyway, and I've got a lot of things to do tomorrow. You go and do what you've got to do. Besides, as you say, 'you're a grown-ass man.' You can do what you want," she said, yawning.

"Cool. I'll try not to be too late."

"Yeah, *right*," Terri replied, knowing that Victor comes home when Victor *wants* to come home.

V reached over to the radio dial and found a station that plays jazz all day on Sundays, but he didn't turn it up too loud because it looked like Terri was trying to get that catnap. He took out a piece of paper that Cassie handed him before he left Moms's. It had a phone number and an address on it.

I don't know either one of these. She could have told me when I was locked up she changed her shit, thought V. The note also said, "Need to see you . . . TONIGHT!" V guessed it meant she wanted to talk or see Victor this same evening. *What reason does she have to see Victor? Hell, should I even go over there?* He didn't want to think the worst, but what could be worse than being accused of something you didn't do? Since he knew he was accused of something and he *knew* he didn't do it, it was only fair *not* to accuse Cassie without proof. V decided to kill two birds with one stone; he would meet with Junior and then see what Cassie was up to. He had this uneasy feeling, but then he *did* just sex his sister-in-law. One thing was for sure: this whole situation was moving too fast too soon, and it had to hurry up and be settled before someone got hurt. V didn't know how much longer he would be able to keep this up.

They pulled up to the front gate of their estate, V said what he had to say to gain access inside, and they were on their way up the long driveway to the garage. V opened up the first door of the garage but didn't pull in.

"Terri? Terri, we're home."

<u>Home.</u> V realized for the first time in a *long* time he hadn't had a place to call home. He was content to stay at Moms's, seeing as how there was no rent to pay. But a home of his *own*, he *never* had. The thought came to him: *If I wanted to, I could just keep on being Vic. I would be living large with a woman who loves me . . . well, him. I could just let the people at the firm run everything. All my money problems would be a thing of the past. I'd be riding* phat *vehicles! This would definitely be the life! Then again,* my name would be tarnished, Victor would be dead, and Moms would figure me out sooner or later. Honestly, I don't want any one of those things to happen. Even Victor's outcome.

Terri yawned, stretched, and unbuckled her seat belt. She was full, and her eyes were heavy. The only thing on her mind was her king-sized bed and plenty of sleep.

"Don't bother waking me when you get back. I know I probably won't see you until tomorrow evening, seeing as how you *always* get up at five thirty in the morning."

Five thirty! V thought, almost saying it out loud.

"Yeah, uh, okay" was all V could come up with. "Call me at work tomorrow. Maybe, if I'm not too busy, we can catch lunch or something. That is, if I don't call you first."

Terri raised an eyebrow.

"Really? Wow! Okay. Wait a minute . . . What do you mean 'or something'?"

V leaned over in the Maybach and gave Terri a short but sweet kiss on the lips. "I mean *lunch*," he said. Terri got out, closed the door, and stood there watching her man drive away. As he got to the edge of the gate, she couldn't help think about the way her husband had been acting since meeting with his twin. It made her smile.

Victor never *asks me if it's okay for him to meet someone. He* never *mentions going out for lunch. And* damn, *he hasn't made love to me like he did last night since . . . hell, I can't remember. Either someone has kidnapped the* real *Victor or he needs to get head-butted more often.*

She shook her head as she went inside, still smiling.

* * *

V drove up to the little restaurant called Joey's. It had a different name years ago: The Piping Pie. He remembered coming here many times to hang out with his boy Junior, just laughing and having a good time. But somehow tonight would not be the same because Junior was under the impression that this was not his homey but rather his homey's brother, the attorney.

I think I'll have some fun, thought V. Junior was already there and had ordered himself a drink. As V walked in, he looked where he and Junior used to sit and was surprised to find Junior in the exact same booth. The only thing that had changed was the scenery. It had autographed pictures of actors and singers all over the place that had come there before. The colors were a light brighter too, with a lot of reds and oranges. As far as where Junior sat, V thought, I *guess some things never change.*

"Well, I can see you're already here," V said.

"Well, I'm actually surprised that *you* came . . .," Junior said, looking at his watch. "And you're on *time* too!"

"You forget I'm *not* my lazy-ass brother."

V could tell that talking down about himself to Junior made Junior squirm in his seat. Junior obviously didn't like it, and that made V feel even better that his best friend held him with such high regard.

"Whatever," Junior responded. "Did you want something to drink? My treat. I just ordered a cream soda, and it looks like it's coming now. If you were V, I would know what to order for you. But since you're not, I haven't a clue."

"*What?* No *liqueur?* You've raised my curiosity! If I *were* V, what would I want?"

Junior thanked the waitress for bringing his drink and took a sip.

"A suicide," Junior replied.

"A *suicide?* I figured he was suicidal, but what the *hell* is a suicide?" V asked, knowing very well what it was and that his friend knew him very well. "Do you think I'd want a drink that would *kill* me?"

"*I would hope* so, but that's not what a suicide is. It's all the soft drinks combined . . . or most of them. You know, Coke, root beer, orange, strawberry, or whatever else he wanted. V liked it like that."

V started grinning. He couldn't keep it in any longer. He wanted to tell someone, and he felt that Junior was the only one would keep his identity a secret. He had to get this off his chest, but now he had to figure out how. He would just have to trust that his homeboy had his back.

* * *

Moms was just getting ready for bed, but she was still wound up from the evening's escapades to go straight to sleep. Pastor Stanley talked about her son Vincent. Terri bragged on *other* son Victor. And Cassie talked about *herself.* After the pastor left, Moms just kept her eyes on everyone. *Who was this* Roger *fellow? Was Terri talking about the same son I knew? Why was Cassandra all ears about Terri's conversation? Why won't Victor look me in the eyes? That* question nagged at her most of all, and it seemed strange to Moms. She felt he was up to something, but she didn't want to accuse. There was enough of *that* already. *Hmmph! The nerve of Pastor to talk about my son! Deep down, he knows it was Vincent who helped him on those hot summer days.* Moms just couldn't get over this thought. Maybe this was what had her so wound up. Maybe it was the fact that she *could have* shot a preacher in her house, even though she didn't fire a shot. *Maybe the reverend has a point, but even if he does, if God ain't given up my son, why should we?* she thought. She grabbed her Bible and started reading Psalms 37: "Fret not thyselves of evildoers . . ." She put the book down, got on the side of her bed, and began to pray.

"Lord, Father God in Heaven. It's me again, your child. I know I done called you many a time in my life. And most times you saw about me and mine. To tell the truth, *every time* you saw about me and mine! And I thank you for everything you done. I still don't understand why you took my man away from me and the boys, but I believe you know what you're doing. Anyway, I'm calling on you again. This time I'm asking for you to shed some light on all this mess. I get this strong feeling that my Vincent didn't do the crime he's being accused of. I don't know who, and I don't know how, but that's how I feel. Please, Lord, don't let my son die for something he didn't do. I *know* he didn't do it! I just *know* it! Shed some light on this and please make everything better. Thank you in advance. In Jesus's name, Amen."

She was about to get up but remembered something else.

"Oh, and I almost forgot. Please forgive me for almost blasting a hole in one of your messengers. Maybe *next* time, he'll watch what he says!"

CHAPTER 20

THREATS AND PROMISES

"The hell with you, Coop! I'm *not* someone's puppet! I don't care *what* or *who* you tell about me and my business! You don't know shit anyway! I've decided that I've run away from being responsible for far too long, and I ain't *running* no more!"

Kevin was giving Cooper an earful. He started feeling like he had lost all control of his life and now would probably be the best time to take back what was lost—his dignity.

"You know *what*, Casey? You just *thought* you were in trouble, but if you think you can sit there and tell *us* what you *will* and *won't* do, then your troubles have just begun, boy!" Cooper said. "I can see that you getting hurt isn't much of a concern of yours. But you forget you've got a daughter that I'm *positive* we can find if we need to."

Kevin jumped up from the bench he was sitting on, grabbed Cooper, and started punching him in the face with all he had. Three other guards had just walked in when they heard the scuffle. They rushed to Cooper's aide, but it wasn't easy pulling Kevin off him. He was a strong one. He was able to get in about nine or ten more punches before he was finally wrestled to the ground.

"I *told* you! Didn't I *tell* you? Don't *fuck* with my daughter! I will *kill* you, you bastard! Do you *hear* me? I'll kill you *dead*, you fucking *bastard*!"

"No, Officer Casey," coming from a voice behind Kevin. It was the warden. "No, I'm afraid you *won't* be making threats like that, and you *sure* won't be able to follow *through* with them. Turn in your equipment. You're *suspended*."

"*What?* But *you* didn't hear him threaten my daughter's *life, did* you?" Kevin said while still being detained by the other guards. "Let me *go,* dammit!"

"You're right, Casey. I *didn't* hear what Officer Cooper said about your daughter. But I did just hear *you* threaten Officer Cooper. And from the looks of things, these men came in here just in the nick of time. Cooper, are you all right?"

"I don't think so, sir," Cooper said weakly.

"Check him out," the warden said to one of the guards. "Officer Casey, with your threatening statements and all the blood on your hands, this could be looked upon as attempted murder. You *know* that, right?"

"Yes, sir, it *could* be looked upon that way. But I wasn't trying to kill him. *Hurt* him? *Hell yeah,* I tried to hurt his ass! I need for him to understand that I mean *business* when it comes to me and mine!"

"Well, I mean business too, and with what you've just done and what you've just said, it doesn't look good for you. Gather up your stuff and hand me your badge. We'll contact you later on what has been decided."

The warden held out his hand, waiting for Kevin to hand him his badge. Kevin stood still, staring at the warden.

"Look, son, you're not being *fired.* Just suspended until we figure this shit out. Come on now. Don't make it any *worse* for you," the warden said.

Cooper had been helped up to a sitting position on the floor with his back against the wall.

"Yeah, grab yo' shit and git the fuck out of here!"

"Shut your ass up, Coop! I'll want a full report of this on my desk first thing in the morning. You *got* that, Officer?"

"Yeah," Cooper answered. "I *got* it."

Kevin was pissed.

"What the *fuck* is this? *He* gets to turn in a report and *I* get *suspended*? What kind of bullshit is *that*?" Kevin asked.

"Watch your mouth and calm down, son. The best thing you can do at *this* moment is acquire you a good lawyer," the warden replied. "Just in case."

"Oh, I *see.* You've already made up your mind as to what my fate is, huh? Well, his ass won't get away with this! I *promise* you that!" He handed the warden his badge and his gun.

"Say, Warden, that sounds like another threat, doesn't it?" Cooper asked.

"As a matter of fact, it *does*. Was that another threat, Officer Casey?" asked the warden.

Kevin was on his way out of the locker room but turned around right at the door.

"It's obvious you sissies ain't *listening* to me. I *said* what I *meant*. That was *not* a threat. *That* was a fucking *promise!*"

Kevin exited out of the room, knocking the door off its hinges.

The warden turned to the other three guards.

"Okay, fellows, you can leave. I'll make sure Coop gets medical attention."

"But I came in here to change," said one of the guards.

"Change later. Right now, I need you . . . to get . . . the fuck . . . out," the warden said decisively. The guards exited, and the warden lit into Cooper.

"You want to tell me what the fuck *that* was all about?"

Cooper was dabbing at his face with a now blood-stained handkerchief. "Our Mr. Casey *suddenly decided* he would no longer do what was *asked* of him. You *do* know what I'm talking about, *right?*"

"Yes, *I* know."

"Well, I know you may have to go through some legal mumbo jumbo, but *I* want revenge! Look at how bad his rusty-ass hands messed up my face!"

"Coop. You are already one *ugly* sumbitch, so if he did *anything* to your face, it was an improvement."

"Kiss my ass, Bill. I'll tell you *this* much. Mr. Casey needs to have a little accident. I don't care what Sabino says!"

"Sabino's *not* the one in charge. Never *has* been. Sure you're probably entitled a little restitution, but unless you get the word from *me*, you cannot touch him. Don't you *kill* him. Understand?"

"Yeah, I understand. Even though he killed my best friend, I won't kill him. I can hurt him without laying a *finger* on him. If I make a phone call to my friends out of town, he'll never see that daughter of his again and he'll only *wish* he were dead."

CHAPTER 21

AND THE WINNER IS . . .

"I think I'll try that suicide," V said to the waitress who stood by just in case he was ready to order. Once she got the different flavors he desired, she hurried off to make the drink. It was near closing time, and she was more than ready to finish her tasks, clean off her areas, and head home.

"Look, I know that you asked to meet with me this evening to discuss some sort of plan to help your ace, *right*?" V said.

"That's right."

The waitress returned to the table with V's drink and winked at him.

"Well, before we do," V said while taking a sip of his drink, "say, this is pretty damn *good*!" he said to the waitress, handing her a $20 bill. "Thanks, sweetie. Keep the change." He turned his attention back to Junior.

"I thought I said 'my treat'?" Junior asked.

"That wasn't anything. You can still give her something, if you like. Anyway, before we discuss anything, let's play a game."

"A *game*? We don't have *time* for no damn games! What *type* of game, anyway?" Junior asked.

"Well, it goes like this. Let's see who can shock the other person the *most*, you know, with some sort of news or info. As soon as we see who is shocked the *most*, we can discuss whatever you'd like. Now I have *never* lost this game. Do you think you're *up* for it?" V asked.

Junior thought to himself for a minute. *What could this fool possibly be up to? Victor never does anything unless it can benefit him. Oh well, I guess it wouldn't hurt if he knew something. Maybe he'll be inclined to help out. Hell, it's all about winning for Victor anyway.*

"Yeah, I'm up for it. Who goes first?"

V looked at his friend and said, "Age before beauty."

Junior didn't like Victor Taylor, and he was now questioning whether discussing *anything* about his friend Vincent was a good idea. He had to try something, however, to help V. Junior started.

"Okay then. You know, as *well* as V, that each year I would make a road trip. I wouldn't say where, not even to my boy V, just in case things *didn't* work out. Well, things *did* work out. As a matter of fact, they worked out even better than I could have imagined. You saw my lady friend today, right? Well, it looks like we *might* get married."

"Yeah, I heard you earlier. *Married*, huh?" V said. This *was* shocking news to V.

"Yeah. Well, I haven't *asked* her yet, but I am. You see, not only are we an item, but we work in the same *profession* as well."

Junior paused.

"Are you *sure* you're ready for this?"

"What? You're *not* finished?" V asked.

"No."

"Okay, then hit me with your *best* shot. You forget, *I'm* the reigning champion of *this* game."

"All right, here goes: I've been traveling to New Orleans, Louisiana, to do extensive training to become an FBI agent. I am now full-fledged, certified, legal, and as a matter of fact, on assignment right now," he said, flashing his badge.

V's mouth flew open. He sat across the table from not only his best friend in the world, but also a certified FBI agent. He reached out for the badge, and Junior handed it to him. All this time wondering where Junior would go, leaving him to deal with life's situations on his own, not calling or writing, only to find out that Junior did something responsible with his life. V was too impressed.

"*Damn!* You're *serious*, aren't you? What about those hustles you'd pull for cash?"

"Just passing the time away. You could take me out of the mischief, but you couldn't take the mischief out of me."

"I'm impressed! FBI? What kind of assignment?"

"I can't tell you that! But seeing as how much this has shocked you, if I'm not *more* shocked than you, then *I* will win this little game of yours."

"I must admit you play it quite *well*! I don't know if I'll be able to *top* that, but I'll give it the old college try."

V looked over his left shoulder and then his right, always trying to build up the suspense. He leaned forward and waited for Junior to do the same, which he did.

V began, "I am not *who* or *what* everybody *thinks* I am."

"Oh, I don't know about *that*. You *are* an asshole, right?" Junior shot back.

"Very funny. *Not.*"

"Okay, I'll play right. So what does that *mean*? You're not a *man*? You're not a *lawy*er? You're not into *women*? *What?*"

It appeared Junior had begun to enjoy this game, especially seeing as how if any one of these questions were answered with a yes, then he would have beaten the *great* Victor Taylor at his own game. None of these things would shock Junior as much as *his* story shocked "Mr. Taylor."

"Well, you're *partly* right. Oh, I'm all man and absolutely *adore* women. But I'm not a lawyer, though, not *really*, that is. No, my shock story is . . . you ready?"

"Oh, I'm *ready*, all right." Junior's eyes were fixed on V.

"I am . . . *not* . . . Victor Taylor."

Junior leaned back in his seat and then leaned forward again, studying the man across the table from him.

"If you're not Victor Taylor, then who the *fuck* am I talking to? You must have a pretty good makeup artist. You *look* like him, you *walk* like him, you *talk* like him, and you *act* like—"

"No makeup artist."

"Well, then who the hell *are* you?" asked Junior "'Cause as far as *I* know, Vincent and Victor are twins and *not* triplets, and Vincent is in jail at the moment on death row!"

"*Is* he now? All I can say is that I absolutely *love* this drink I ordered. Want to know something else? I've *always* loved it . . . all my life."

Junior looked even harder at V. You could practically hear his heart thumping, and you could smell the machinery going on inside his head.

"*Wait* a minute! Are you trying to tell me that *you're Vincent? V,* is that *you?*"

V knew that only one word would win this game for him, and it was now time to say it.

"Yes. It's me."

There was that awkward silence that these men shared when you don't quite know what to say next or if you should say anything at all. However, Junior finally broke the quietude.

"Naw, naw, it just *can't* be! Who do you think you're trying to fool? I don't think you understand. I work for the FBI! You can't pull no juvenile shit like this on *me*! Deductive reasoning asks the question, if *you* are V, then where is *Victor*? Tell me *that*, smartass."

"Where I *left* him. In *prison*."

"*Bullshit!* Victor wasn't the one arrested in the *first* place, was he?"

V shook his head no.

"Still, you *can't* be V because V would have asked me to help him."

Junior was in denial, but who could blame him? If the last bit of news about your best friend was that he was on death row, in prison, with no outside help, how then could he possibly be sitting right across you in a restaurant? Experience told Junior that when a scam was worked up by these two, V would set it up, and Junior would set it off. He just sat there trying to think of a way that V, Victor, or whoever this man was could prove that what he was saying was true.

"I *couldn't* ask you to help. I wasn't in the *position* to ask you to help. Hell, I didn't even know where you *were*!"

"You know what?" asked Junior. "I ought to shoot you right where you're sitting. I am *strapped*, you know."

"Yeah, I know *you* are. But am *I*? You don't really *know* that, do you? But why shoot *me*?"

"Why? Because you know how close V and I are, and you just can't *stand* it! You haven't even *tried* to lift a finger to help him, and now he's on lockdown for something that probably doesn't even *concern* him! So I guess if you play this little joke on me, it makes you feel like some kind of *big man* or something."

V just smiled.

"*Emotional*, aren't we? Listen, man. What if I *can* prove I'm Vincent?" he asked.

"*Prove* it, punk! I'm listening. But if you don't convince me, I just may have to do some paperwork . . . on a 187."

"Yeah, but you may want to pull a 120 because you may be dealing with a 133. I *know* you are familiar with those terms, right?"

"Yeah, I know them. How do you?"

"You forget . . . I've been in prison, and I read. I've made stupid mistakes, but I'm not stupid."

"Okay. I hear you. Prove it."

"Ah-ight. Kool. No problem. Do you remember when we were in high school, we had a little saying? We were the *only* ones who knew it. Right?"

"V and *I* had a saying. I remember it, but even if you know it, how do I know V didn't just tell it to you?" Junior asked.

"First of all, let me tell you what *happened* and *why* we came up with it, and *then* you decide. Remember that one time we covered for your uncle? He was coming out of Baby Love's house, and we were coming back from a party. Aw yeah, he was busted, ah-ight. He was supposed to be all *military* and *loyal* to his country and your auntie. We could have told *everything*, but he begged us not to and promised you he'd *never* do it again. Remember *that*? You *do* remember Baby Love, right? That *pretty* hoe."

"Yeah," Junior said, smiling, "she *was* fine! *Too* fine to be *selling* her body. What happened to her anyway? Didn't she become a lot lizard? Is she still around?"

"Naw, she got religious. Joined church. Turned her life around. Last I heard, she was some kind of traveling *evangelist*, saving souls for God. I saw her right before she left. She *still* looked good! *Damn* good, if I can say that about a preacher!"

"Well, that *is* good news. I guess *anybody* can change, huh? Anyway, yeah. I remember that night. That was only shared by me, my uncle, and V."

"That is *correct*, sir. Do you think that V would tell *Victor* this information, very well knowing that Victor would *probably* extort your uncle for money or other favors?"

"I *know* he wouldn't."

"Damn *straight*. Ready for the saying we made up that night?"

"As corny as it is . . . if you know it, then say it."

V started, "My friend to the end. You can always call . . ."

Junior joined him to finish the last part of their made up saying.

"All for one . . . and one for all," they said together.

"*Damn! V!* It's really *you*, isn't it? But *how?*" asked Junior in as much awe as in shock of the situation.

"Close your mouth, dude. You about to slobber. Do you remember the TV show *Hee Haw*?"

"Yeah. What about it?"

"They had a segment on there with these women. I'm going to steal one of their lines: 'You'll never hear one of us repeating gossip.' So you better be sure and listen close the first time."

V began to tell his longtime friend every detail about how, who, what, when, and where, even *why*, but stopped when he thought maybe they should meet up at a more discreet location, like at the Taylor firm. Junior was very relieved and glad to see his old compadre. These one-time boys, who grew up to be young men, knew a plan *had* to be put into action.

"Oh. By the way . . . *who* just won the little game we just played?" V asked.

"Shut up!" Junior answered.

CHAPTER 22

NEW SHIT

V pulled up to the high-rise apartment complex and checked the address to the note Cassie gave him. It matched. He dialed the new number, just in case she didn't want to be bothered. It was already 12:15 a.m., and V didn't *even* think about calling *before* he went over there.

"Hello?"

"Cassandra? This is Victor. I'm outside in the parking deck. You still want to see me?"

"Sure do! Come on up. I'll buzz you in."

V entered the front of the apartments and walked straight until he reached a gold-plated elevator. *Cassie can't afford a place like this!* he thought. *Is she hoe-ing?*

As he got off the elevator and walked down the hall leading to her room, there were paintings of an up-and-coming local artist draped on both sides of the walls. The smell of jasmine and clean laundry permeated the air. The carpeted floors looked as if they were recently vacuumed. The rooms were spaced so far apart that there couldn't have been more than ten rooms total on each floor.

"Hey, baby!" Cassie greeted V with a grin and then a kiss. She wore a sheer Victoria's Secret robe and had on some Angel perfume, the kind that said, "Come and get me!" She grabbed him by the hand and led him into her plush suite. The place was decorated with black leather furniture with soft white chemise draped over them, marble and pewter coffee and end tables, a lion-skin rug on the floor in front of a blazing fireplace, black-and-white photos of famous black movie stars hung on every wall.

V was taken aback, seeing as how he knew how Cassie was living *before* he went in prison, living in a tiny apartment close to his home.

"I am *so* glad to see you! But I am a little pissed right now," she said with pouty lips.

V wasn't quite sure if she was referring to *him* or Victor. He couldn't tell if she knew the difference right now.

"Why are you pissed at *me*? What did *I* do?"

"You left town and didn't even tell me. I had to go and visit your brother in prison and you're off gallivanting somewhere else."

"Say my name," V said. "My *whole* name."

"Victor Latrell Taylor. You are so damned *conceited*. Now *why* did I have to do *that*, boo?"

Damn, she does *think I'm Victor!*

"I'm not conceited. I'm *convinced*! *Why?* Do I ever give you a reason as to *why* I do things?"

"Not really. Did you just hear me say that I was *pissed* at you?"

"Get over it. I'm here *now*, aren't I?"

"Yeah, but . . . I know. It had something to do with our *plans*, didn't it?"

"*What* plans? I have so many plans going on at the same time I don't have a clue as to what you're *talking* about."

V was going to let Cassie fill him in on what was going on. He didn't know what Victor had his hands in. This was all about remaining focused on the task he had to deal with. He was, however, hurt at the moment and pissed off *himself*.

"*You* know, the $5 million plan that you included me in. We're *still* going to be together when all this is over with, aren't we?"

"Yeah, you know it. Say, do you have something to drink?"

"What you *want*, sugar?"

"Fix me a cognac."

She didn't move. V just looked straight in her eyes. "Fix me a goddamn cognac . . . please." At first, Cassie got a little scared but then calmed down and returned his fixation with a mischievous smile. She stepped out of the room to her kitchen to fix a couple of drinks. V found this as an opportunity to peruse the apartment. He looked on shelves, hoping to find something, anything with a name or address or number. The thing that stood out was a stereo system he only could *dream* of owning and some mini cassettes labeled with some sort of code.

"Make yourself at home. Have a seat. I'll be in there in a minute," Cassie called out from the other room.

V took one of the cassettes and put it in his pocket. Cassie entered.

"I see you've found my tapes. Remember what I told you before? I record *all* conversations I'm in earshot of. That's all of them right there."

"So how do I know you're not recording what we say right *now*?" V asked.

"You *don't*. But I'm *not*. Here's your drink."

V took a long sip. He was trying to process what was going on.

"Now . . . are you going to *kiss* me or what?"

V was pissed, but he wasn't stupid. He knew what it felt like to kiss her, hold her, and be inside of her. He pulled her close to him and kissed her passionately, so much that she became moist between her legs.

"Oh, *Victor*! *Sex* me!"

He reached his hand down and began to rub on her V-jay jay and then suddenly stopped. He just couldn't get past the fact that she called him Victor.

"I can't *do* this."

"Why *not*? I *want* you."

V composed himself before answering that question. He couldn't believe that his brother and his supposedly girlfriend were having an *affair*. As much as he wanted to lay her down, he wanted to slap the *shit* out of her too.

"Look, I promised Terri I'd be home at a decent hour tonight. You know as well as I do, if we are truly going to be together in our 'plans,' then we are going to have to play it cool, right?"

Cassie pouted again. "*Shit*. Okay. But I don't like it. Damn, boy, you got me all hot and shit. You *do* realize it's no longer night, don't you? Hell, you've *already* missed your curfew."

"Girl, I don't have a *fucking* curfew! I can do—"

"Take your ass home, Victor. I can't stand for you to stay here any longer. If you do, I'm going to pull out all the stops and you *will* be staying. Long enough to get some of this ass!"

When he looked at Cassie, he *almost* changed his mind. She was fine, and he missed her, but obviously, she didn't miss *him*. Besides, he became increasingly angry the more he thought about Victor boning his girl. But then again, maybe she was never *his* in the first place. How long has this *really* been going on? V gulped down his drink, hoping it would numb some of the pain and shock he was experiencing. He headed for the door but turned quickly.

"You know, Cassie, you should really put those tapes up in a safer place than that. As a matter of fact, let me borrow a couple. I need to make sure there are no slip ups."

"Sure, Victor. I'll do *anything* for you . . . *even* if you won't do *anything* for me," she said while touching herself between her thighs. She pulled off her robe to reveal even *more* of what she had in store for "Victor." She walked over to the shelf where the tapes were, trying to find the ones she felt would be of most importance to him. Looking at her from behind, V found himself uncontrollably moving toward her. He reached around Cassie and cupped her breasts, fondling her nipples and kissing on her neck. She turned around, kissed him, and started to unzip his pants.

"*No!* I mean, *damn*, girl, you feel *good*, no doubt. But if I'm going to *do* you, then I'm going to do you *right*, and right now, I *know* I don't have that kind of time. I gotta go. Sorry."

"I understand, but like I said, I don't like it! You got me all horny, and I *knew* I should have bought that BOB when I had the chance! Here. These tapes ought to catch you up. Hell, I thought you were on your game. What happened to the *great* Victor Taylor?"

She handed him three tapes. That makes four total.

"Oh, you hadn't heard? Got head-butted by your *boyfriend* Saturday morning. But I'll have to catch you up on that later. Look, I'll make it up to you. I promise."

"Um hmm. Bye, Victor. *Bastard.*"

"What did you say? Watch your mouth, you hear?"

"Sorry."

V headed for the door again.

"Say, Victor."

"Yeah."

"Thanks for buying me this place. I *love* it! If you give me the chance, I'll thank you *properly* later."

"No problem, Cassandra. I'm going to *hold* you to that!"

V closed the door behind him and heard the locks being utilized as he walked toward the elevator.

You ain't never *gonna get no more of* this *dick! And I'm going to kick Victor's ass!* he thought as he waited for the elevator to open. As the doors opened, he said, "No, I'm not. I'm gonna fuck his *wife's* brains out!" A well-dressed elderly woman was just exiting the elevator as he made that statement. She looked at him with disgust as he got on.

"Practicing my lines for a play," he offered her as an explanation right before the doors closed.

Cassie picked up her phone, punched digits, and waited for an answer on the other end.

A groggy voice answered. "Hello?"

"Hey, Roger. Do you remember how you said you would *hook* me up if I hooked *you* up? *Yeah?* You still *got* that? Well, come on over, hon. This is your *lucky* day!"

CHAPTER 23

INTERMISSION

Knock. Knock.
Junior was knocking on the bedroom door where Patricia was. "Patricia?" he whispered. "Say, Pat."

Patricia opened the door, wearing a cute little teddy that at any other time would have said, "Come and get me, lover!" But Junior knew this was neither the time nor the place to be trying anything on a sexual tone. It didn't help matters she was so fine.

"What's up, baby? Is everything all right?" she asked.

"It's even better now that I've seen you! Damn, I miss you!"

"I miss you too. That's why I have plans for us tomorrow. Now don't start playing detective with me 'cause you *know* it won't work, don't you?"

Junior liked the games Pat played with him. Just thinking about what she had in mind made his "nature" rise.

"Yeah, okay. Look, we need to talk. Are you super sleepy?"

"Naw." She yawned.

"Good. Grab a robe and meet me in the kitchen."

Junior went down to the kitchen and grabbed a couple of bottles of spring water from the fridge. He opened his and took a long gulp, and by the time he opened hers, she entered the room.

"Now tell me, what could be *so* important you couldn't let me finish getting my beauty sleep?"

"Baby, you don't even *need* beauty sleep. Your beauty is always on automatic!"

Patricia smiled. It felt good to have a man that appreciated and expressed approval of her looks. She didn't doubt herself as being good-looking, but she was not the type of person that pointed this fact out to anyone.

"Anyway," she said, blushing.

"*Anyway*. What did you think of our Victor Taylor when you guys met?"

"Honestly, I felt he was stuck on himself. He's cute. Quite handsome, really. You say Vincent is his identical? I hope his attitude is better because Victor's attitude made him very unattractive. You two don't see eye to eye all that much."

Junior smiled. "No, *Victor* and I *don't* see eye to eye. I know you didn't really know how the brothers acted, but I'll tell you this much: The way you witnessed Victor's behavior is the way Victor *always* behaves. He was just typical."

"So what did you and Victor come up with to help V? Did you tell him why *we* were here? To find answers about a cocaine ring?"

"Naw, it wasn't any of his business. Besides, we may have to put *that* on hold for a minute anyway. I've found out something else."

"What's that?" she asked, taking a sip of water.

"Are you ready for this? Our friend Victor Taylor is *really* Vincent! Girl, that's *V!*"

"Wait a minute! Let me see if I understand correctly. Victor Taylor, the lawyer, whom I met at your mom's, was *not Victor Taylor*? So *Vincent Taylor*, who is supposed to be locked up and on death row, was sitting at the kitchen table?"

Junior just smiled and nodded.

"So that would mean that the *real* Victor Taylor is in *prison*?"

"Damn, girl! Quit it! You're just *too* smart!"

"No, *you* quit it! What do we do *now*? If V is *already* out, what *else* is there for us to do? He doesn't need help getting out if he's *already* out."

"It's still *his* identity that's in question. If we don't help prove that V is truly innocent of the accused crime, then Victor will still be executed, and V will have to live with that . . . hell, so will *I*!"

"How can you be so sure he was *not* Victor trying to play you? Did he have *proof*?"

"He *did*, trust me. The more we talked, the more I *knew* it was V! You know, he switched places with his brother! Ha, ha, ha!"

"What? Victor just *let* him switch places with him?"

Junior gave the you-gotta-be-kidding look.

117

"Yeah, *right*. Victor, who happens to hate the ground that V walks on, says to him, 'Oh sure, I'll be *glad* to switch places so you can clear your name.' Trust me, *that* would *never* happen."

"Okay, so I'll ask you again. What do we do *now*?"

"We just lay low for a couple of days, but we keep our ears and eyes open for *anything*. We've got to let V get his feet wet at Victor's firm. He said to look forward to hearing from him by Wednesday or Thursday. He and I talked, but you're my *partner*, so is that *cool* with you?"

Pat looked at Junior with bedroom eyes, grabbed his hand, and said, "That's *more* than cool with me. Just don't *think* of making any plans tomorrow. Day *or* night!"

CHAPTER 24

WRONG FLOOR

Riiinggg! The alarm clocked startled Vincent. He had only gotten four hours of sleep and was tired as hell, but he figured he'd better get up, get dressed, and get down to the *office*—his *brother's* office, his *own* office. Didn't matter *how* you looked at it now, Vincent Taylor was now Victor Taylor. He didn't bother Terri; he just let her lay there knocked out.

Let's see. What should I wear today? Vincent thought as he rifled through Victor's suits. *Well now,* this *is nice!* Victor found a nice brown Bill Blass ensemble with matching shoes and decided to wear it.

"Damn, I look good! Vic sure knows how to dress. Thanks again, bro."

V headed downstairs, grabbed the keys to the Ferrari, and got ready to head to "his" office.

"Dammit, I almost forgot! Gotta grab those tapes and have someone pick me up a mini-cassette player."

He reached in the Maybach and picked up the tapes he left in the glove compartment, jumped in the car, and headed down the winding driveway. The ride to work was quiet with not much traffic to get in his way.

"Uh huh, beat the *rush*, didn't I?" he said proudly. "But then coming in from this way, there's probably not going to *be* much of a rush. Anyways, with this here phat ride, I'm gonna fly past *anyone* going too slow!"

Hell, everyone's *going to be driving too slow this morning,* he thought.

When he got to his brother's building, he found just what he thought he'd find: a parking space especially "designed" for Victor Taylor. It said, "Big Boss's Space. All others will be towed."

Egomaniac, he thought to himself.

As he entered the building, he was greeted with the "normal" "Hello, Mr. Taylor" and "Morning, sir" from the workers who were already there.

Damn, these people start early! he thought.

As he approached the elevator, he stopped to look at the board that told where all the offices were located. There was no sense in getting on the elevator, not knowing where he was going. A young man walked up on him from behind and pushed the up button on the elevator.

"Admiring the details, sir?"

"Uh yes, by the way, I was. You *do* have something to do today, don't you?"

"Oh yes, sir. I'm working on a case now that will probably go to court this week."

"Good. Come see me this morning at about nine."

"At nine? Yes, sir, I'll be there. What's it about?"

V just looked at him.

The elevator doors opened, and both men got on board.

"Sorry, sir. Never mind. I'll be there. Nine o'clock. Nice suit, sir."

"Thanks. Are you sucking up to me?"

The man blushed. "No, sir! I just notice nice things, that's all."

"Good. But don't ever do that again. I don't like it."

"Yes, sir. Um, excuse me, sir, are you telling me not to notice nice things or not to suck up?"

"What I'm telling you is not to be a dumbass or a wiseass, but you should be able to figure out what I meant in the beginning. Are you sure you're an attorney of mine?"

"Yes, sir! I *fully* understand what you meant."

"Good." *Because I didn't,* V thought to himself.

V and the young gentleman were quiet the rest of the ride until the doors opened on the fifth floor. The man got off.

"Nine o'clock," V said.

"Yes, sir, I'll be there."

Before the doors closed, a woman was rushing to get on the elevator.

"Could you hold the doors, please?" she said, trying to get on. V held the doors as she entered.

"Good morning," he offered.

"Good morning. Wow, I got off on the wrong floor. I'm trying to apply for a job here. Wow, you look *nice*! This is a nice *place*! Are the people friendly here? Do you happen to know Mr. Victor Taylor personally? I'm sorry . . . My name is Belinda. Belinda Jett. My mama says I talk too much waaay too soon. Whew, I'm already tired!"

"Yes, you have a very smart *mother*. I *would* shake your hand, but you seem to have your hands full at the moment. Do you need some help?"

"No, I have it."

"So have you ever *seen* Mr. Taylor?" V asked.

"You probably won't believe this, but no, I haven't. All I've done is heard of his reputation as being one of the best defense lawyers in the country. You'd think I'd seen him on TV or something, huh? Guess I was not much into TV or anything else if it didn't pertain to my classes. Anyway, if I'm going to be the best, I feel I should work with the best. Don't you agree?"

"Makes sense to me."

"I finished first in my class in the Duke University Law Department, and well, I guess I wanted to continue to be the best I could be, which brought me here. They have one opening that they are trying to fill, and I sure would like to fill it. You must hold some position here, huh? Dressing all *fancy* and stuff. You look *nice*! I didn't catch your name. You are . . . ?" she inquired.

The doors of the elevator opened up at the tenth floor, and V got off first.

"This is my *floor*," he said.

"*Mine* too! Don't know how I got five and ten mixed up. Guess I'm a little excited."

The receptionist behind the desk greeted him.

"Morning, Mr. Taylor."

"Morning . . ." V glanced quickly at the name plate on the top of the desk.

"Lisa," he continued.

Belinda stopped dead in her tracks.

"You're Mr. Taylor?" she said a little embarrassed.

"Yes," V said with a sly grin. "I guess I'll be seeing you in a little bit, Ms. . . . uh . . ."

"Jett." She gulped. "Belinda Jett."

"That's right. Ms. Jett." V walked away headed toward "his" office.

"Nice talking to you, sir," she called out to him.

V never turned around to acknowledge her. He just opened his door, went in, and closed it behind him. By now, he was laughing.

"That was *funny!*" he said. *She was cute. Vic probably wouldn't even think of hiring her because she didn't even know who he was. But if Vincent has anything to do with it, she's already hired,* he thought.

V went and sat behind the desk. *Hell, now what do I do?*

He pushed the intercom button to reach out to "his" secretary.

"Lisa?"

"Yes, Mr. Taylor?"

"Get my wife on the phone. And let me know when that attorney of mine gets here at nine."

* * *

Kevin was staring out of his bedroom window. He just couldn't sleep. Anxious. Nervous. Debra woke out of her sleep to see Kevin just staring.

"Kevin? What's wrong, baby?" she asked, concerned.

"Nothing . . . just thinking."

"About *what*?"

"Oh, a lot of things. My job . . . my life . . . the future . . . *us*."

"What *about* us? Are you *leaving* me or something?" Debra got worried.

"Naw, naw, nothing like that. If anything, I'm trying to make things better for us. Just give me a little while, I'll tell you about it, okay?"

"Okay." She didn't like it, but she wouldn't pressure Kevin to talk. She was very supportive and loved him with all her heart. She was just waiting for the ultimate commitment to be made to her.

"I gotta go," Kevin said, getting dressed in street clothes.

"You ain't working today?" she asked.

"Naw. I took some time off," he lied while still putting on his shoes. "I'll be back shortly. I love you."

"I love you too, boo."

Kevin kissed Debra on the cheek and then left but didn't really know *where* he was going. He *felt* he knew what he was doing. He just needed to be somewhere where he could think about the *next* step he would take. And he knew *just* the person he needed to see to help him.

CHAPTER 25

PUT INTO ACTION

Victor woke up and stretched. He was not a happy camper, seeing as how he was serving a "special room" sentence that he knows belonged to someone else or no one else. He just knew *he* shouldn't be serving it. He was starting to grow facial hair, and he didn't like *that* either. He did know, however, that when he got out of prison, he was going to kick V's ass, even if it meant he had to sneak up on him. He had no doubts that once he got out of solitary confinement, he would have the resources to get him out of this place. Sure, at first, it may be hard to convince someone that he was not V, but he just had a gut feeling that he would produce the evidence needed to set *him* free.

Bastard! he thought about his brother.

"Guard! Guard! Somebody! Anybody! *Answer* me, damnit!" he yelled from his cold cell.

"Yeah, *yeah*, what *is* it?"

It was Cooper.

"How much longer do I *have* in this shithole?"

"Well, you have been strangely acting in a pretty good manner, so believe it or not, *I've* requested that you only serve two weeks instead of three. There are no promises, but it's better than nothing, right? How does that sound?"

"Again, I say, what choice do I have?"

"Damn, you've even gotten *smarter*! Yeah, you *have* no choice. But you make sure you tell your brother that I was *decent* to you, okay?"

"And what's your name again?"

"Boy, he hit you pretty *hard*, didn't he? The name's Cooper. Jebediah Cooper. Got it?"

123

"Yes, I have it. Say, wasn't there a black guard by the name of Casey that used to work here? What happened to *him*?"

"Oh, Kevin Casey? He was given a little leave. Funky attitude. But we're fixing it for him. He'll be back in a little bit. Why do you ask? You *miss* him, right? I can't believe you can't remember anyone. That's gonna hurt *his* feelings too, you know. I couldn't give a *damn* if you forget my name. Sorta hoping we never met. Anyway, I can't stand around here talking to you all damn day. Your breakfast will be here shortly, but I won't be bringing it. Got shit to do, so you can go back to jacking off!"

"Say, can I get a razor to shave my face?" Victor called out.

"Hell, *naw*!" Cooper said as he walked away.

"Well, *fuck* you then!" Victor yelled out. He didn't want to get into any more trouble than he was in, but he was getting fed up with this "Cooper" person. He figured that Cooper really didn't like V and that it was Kevin that set up the meeting, so it would be Kevin that would be someone to help him get what he needed to make his freedom a reality. He never figured that he would finally understand what his brother was going through in this hellhole. One thing for sure, being on death row was truly a scary experience.

Well, I can't say I don't know what it feels like to be behind bars. Hell, I even understand why V wanted out. I just hope he truly is trying to clear his name because if he doesn't, I could be a dead MF! I truly hate to say this, but now I'm ready to help his ass! Because helping him helps me!

* * *

The phone was ringing at Sabino's office as he was just unlocking the door. He hurried around to the other side of the desk to answer it before the caller hung up.

"Hello?"

"Sabino? This is the colonel. You alone?"

"Yeah, hold on. Let me close this door."

He put down the receiver and walked over to shut and lock his door. He came back and sat in his big office chair.

"Okay, I'm back. How's it going, Colonel?"

"I *could* complain, but no one would listen. However, I need *you* to listen to *me*."

"I'm listening."

"All right. It's time to put everything into action. Is your crew ready?"

"We *will* be. I'm going to—"

"What the fuck? What do you mean 'you *will* be'? It's *time*, gaddamnit! Let's *roll*!"

Sabino loosened the tie he had on.

"I'm gonna need about a month or so to make sure everything goes smoothly. Now you don't want anything to go *wrong*, do you?"

"No. No, I guess not. Okay. You do what you need to do to make this happen and everyone involved will be so fucking *rich* we'll have to buy our own islands for places to stay! Now I can count on you, right?"

"Yeah, Colonel, you can count on me. You *are* sure this is gonna work, right?" Sabino asked.

"It's a little *late* to be asking that *now*, don't you *think*? We've been putting this shit together for years to make sure all players are in place. Now if all the players are *not* in place, two things are sure to happen. First thing, no one will know anything about *me* or that I even existed . . . well, maybe you. But that won't matter . . . not if you talk. And second, even though you are the *only* one who knows who I am, it *will* be you that will go to jail for a very long time. I've made some moves *too*, you know. Now *I'm* ready and you need to *get* ready. We've waited long enough, and I know we have enough involved to make this a reality. Now am I right or am I wrong?"

"You're *right*, Colonel. You are *so* right. Let's do this and get *paid*!"

"Now *that's* what I like to hear. I expect a call back from you in about a *week*, and you had *better* be moving toward being ready in a month's time or less. *Got* it?"

"*Got* it."

"Good."

With that, the colonel hung up the phone without a good-bye. Sabino sat back in his chair and lit up a cigar. He picked up the phone and called his most trusted soldiers.

"Marco? I need for you and Alfonso to make a couple of pick-ups for me. Bring them here next Sunday at noon. *Capisce* . . . ? *Who* . . . ? I'll tell you later when you bring me lunch . . . *Huh?* Hell, *I* don't care! Pick me up something from McAlister's . . . *Damnit*, I know that's not *Italian* food! That's what I have a *taste* for, okay? And make sure you get me one of those salads on the side . . . All right then, see you later."

CHAPTER 26

LUNCH DATE

"Lisa, get me Judge Campbell on the phone, please," V spoke over the intercom. He had been at work for two and a half weeks and still kept forgetting to call this man. He did have lunch with his wife this past Monday, which turned out to be quite interesting.

"Well, well, you *actually* called me for lunch! I'm shocked!" Terri said as she ate her salad.

"Yeah, well, maybe I'm a changed man," V said.

"*Changed* ain't even the word. You're *different*. In a good sort of way, I must say. I *thoroughly enjoyed* Saturday night! Boy, you were most *definitely* the man! I didn't know you knew the positions you put down on me! Have you been studying some sort of manual or watching some porn without me?" she said teasingly.

"I'll *never* divulge my secrets," V said while winking at Terri.

"I *like* McAlister's. *You?*" she asked.

"It's cool. I like the *company*."

"Aw, you say the nicest things on Tuesdays."

"But this is *Monday*, Terri."

"I know."

"You're crazy, you *know* that?"

"I know."

V was actually enjoying the time he was spending with Terri. He found her to be quite fun and full of life. It was invigorating and intoxicating. Not only was she fine, but she was playful as well. He was also enjoying his meal. Nothing like eating out on someone *else's* money. He took a sip of the sweet tea when he noticed someone coming toward his table. Someone he knew. It was Kevin Casey. He almost spoke to him but had to reel himself back in. That would have *surely* blown his cover.

"Mr. Taylor? Hey, do you remember me? I'm the security guard that took you to see your brother Kevin *Casey*."

"*Yes*, Officer Casey. I *do* remember. How *are* you?"

"I'm okay. Look, I hate to bother you, but I was wondering if I could have a minute of your time."

"Well, as you can see, I'm having lunch with my wife. Terri, this is Officer Kevin Casey. Officer Casey, my wife Terri."

"Pleased to meet you, sir," Terri said.

"The pleasure is all mine, Mrs. Taylor. Okay, Mr. Taylor, I see that you're busy. Can I make an appointment then? I need to get some legal paperwork together, and I was wondering if you could be of assistance."

"You *do* realize that I am a defense attorney, right? How do you think I can help you if you're not a *criminal*? Or at least *accused* of committing a crime."

"Sorry. You're right. I'm no criminal, but I will probably need some defense and protection. I'm sorry to have bothered you." Kevin started to walk away from the table.

"Officer Casey."

"Yes, sir?"

"What happened to your hands?" V asked.

"I had to put them on someone."

"Oh. How come you're not at work?"

"Got some leave."

"Okay. Do you think you can be at my office this Friday, say around ten o'clock?"

"Yes, sir. I'll be there."

"Good. We'll talk and let me see what I can do. If I have to, I'll have one of my assistants assist you. How does that sound?"

"Sounds okay to me. That is, if your assistant is as good as you are."

"Hell, son, there's no one as good as I!" V responded. "But you can be sure we'll do you right."

"Already. See you Friday then," Kevin said.

Kevin then took his leave and exited the restaurant, but as he was leaving, he had to step aside for two big guys with leather jackets on to come in. They went to the counter and made an order. One of them looked around the room and spotted V and Terri at their table. He hunched the other guy to look that way. They kept looking until V made eye contact with them. They both gave a two-finger salute to V as if they knew him. V had never seen them before, so he looked over his shoulder to see if they were speaking to someone else, but there was no one behind him. He threw his head back, acknowledging them. They got their order and then left. V and Terri finished up their lunch, and he took out $50 and left it on the table for a tip. V and Terri's entire meal didn't even *come* to $50. As he kissed Terri on the cheek at the door of the restaurant, V told Terri to go on to her car and that he had forgotten something at the table. He walked back up to the counter.

"Uh, excuse me. Do you know who those two guys were that was just in here?"

"Yeah, just about everyone knows Alfonso and Marco! You know Sabino, right? Those are his main muscle. You know, the *punishers*?"

"Oh yeah, I *thought* they looked familiar. I just wanted to make sure. Hadn't seen them in a while," he lied.

V then left the restaurant, got in his car, and headed back to the office.

Oh shit, he thought. *I wonder what Victor has gotten himself mixed up with.*

* * *

"Judge Campbell? Victor Taylor. Hey, look, I know you're a busy man but . . . Well, I need for you to get a message to the warden . . . What's the *message*? Well, if you give me a goddamn minute, I'll tell you. It's 'Free Pee Wee Sea . . . ?' Yeah, write it down . . . Yeah, just like that but add a question mark. Right . . . Okay, you *got* it . . . ? No, *sea.* S, E, A . . . All right, so how will I know you *did* this . . . ? Yes, *that'll* work. Have him call and leave a message with my secretary that he got it, but more important than that is that he *did* it . . . Yeah. Yeah . . . Hell, you *know* I did! Ha ha! That's some funny shit right there . . . Okay. Maybe . . . Well, I don't know about *selling* it. We'll see . . . All right, you too. Good-bye."

V leaned back into his chair, feeling a sense of accomplishment. He finally delivered Pee Wee's message, hired Ms. Belinda Jett, and so far, has fooled everyone into believing he was Victor. He did have one question though: Was he any closer to proving his innocence?

"You the *shit*, man!" he said to himself. "But it's time to get to the *bottom* of this! Talking about *selling it? Really?"*

CHAPTER 27

WANT SOME MORE?

"So how was *that*, baby?" Patricia asked while wrapping the sheet around her.

"That was *fantastic*, babe! Felt like the very *first* time!" Junior responded.

"*Oh*, so it made you feel like a *virgin*? Touched for the very first time?" she teased.

"No, silly ass. It felt like the very first time for you and me. You *must* admit *I* put it down too!"

"Yes, *sir*! You *definitely* put it down! How do you like this *room* I found?"

"It's nice. I *guess*. Hell, I haven't even had a chance to *look* at it. You were on me like a *tiger*, girl!"

"You *like* it, and you *know* it. I *missed* you, boo. Besides, I wanted to be with my man . . . *sexually*, that is."

"That's probably the sweetest thing you could have said to me. So I'm your *man*, huh?"

"Stop *fishing*! You *know* you are. I *love* you."

"I love you *too*. Go take a shower. You've got 'stuff' all over you. Ha!"

"What? Don't you want some *more*?"

"Do *you*?"

"Hell *yeah*!"

"Then why are we talking? Get over here, girl, and let Daddy do you."

"Yes, *sir*."

* * *

V was in the study in "his" house, listening to the tapes that he had gotten from Cassie's place. It was Saturday, and he didn't have anywhere to be, so he thought he'd do some research. He had his headphones on and was facing the door in case Terri walked in on him. He had a little time before she would because she said she had to pick up some things from the store. For some reason, she felt like cooking V a special dinner. V didn't mind, of course. He looked at the calendar and noticed that a full week had past, and although he got the ball rolling on *some* things, he didn't feel like he had found anything that would help him clear his name. *Sexually*, he couldn't complain. If he just *looked* at Terri a certain way, he would be all up *in* her. He thought it was amazing how she didn't say anything about it being so much different from her real husband. He guessed that he and Victor had similar styles. Or maybe she just *liked* the change.

Naw, I've got to be better than him! He chuckled to himself.

Suddenly, V sat straight up in his chair. He heard something on this particular tape that caught his attention that he felt it might be something to share with Junior. He pulled out his iPhone and called his boy.

"Yo, Junior. This is V. I think I found something you can use."

"What is it?" Junior asked.

"I'd rather not say over the phone. Can we meet?"

"Well, I'm sort of in the middle of something right now."

"Oh, sexing *Patricia*, huh?"

"*What? Damn*, man, that's *really* none of your business, dude!"

"Ha ha! Maybe *I* should be the FBI agent. Hell, fool, how long have we known each other? You already *knew* I *already* knew."

"*Bastard*. Okay, you're right. Oooo! Look, man, can I call you back when I finish?"

"You mean, when *I* finish with *you*!" Patricia said in the background.

"Oh shiit!" Junior said with painful pleasure.

"Damn! Ain't no shame in 'nam one of y'all's game, huh? Look, man, call me when you're done. This shit ain't no fun without the video. Ha ha! Later, dude."

"Uh huh. Ughhh!" Junior responded, trying not to scream out over the phone.

V hung up to spare Junior some dignity, but in reality, V was a little jealous.

Hell, I don't know why I'm jealous because my boy is being pleasured. I can't complain. Shit, I'm getting mine. I guess all I can do now is wait until he gets back with me, he thought.

While in mid-thought, his phone rang. He answered without looking, thinking that it's Junior.

"Damn, man, *that* was quick!"

"What the *fuck* you mean? This *Victor*?"

"Yeah. Who is *this*?" V realized it's not his friend.

"This is Marco. The boss wants to see you *tomorrow*."

V realized it's one of the goons he saw at lunch the other day. Even though V personally did not know these guys, he couldn't let it seem like Victor didn't know them.

"The *boss*? Who is . . . okay. But on a *Sunday*? But I was going to church tomorrow," V lied.

"Well then, *that's* where we will pick you up at. Stanley's church, right? Eleven thirty. Don't make us come there and you not be there. This shit ain't funny, and we *definitely* won't be laughing. Be there *this* Sunday for us to pick you up, or be there *next* Sunday being rolled down the aisle."

"I'll be there. So you do know who you're addressing, don't you?"

"Yeah," Marco answered, "a dead motherfucker if he ain't at church tomorrow."

With that being said, the phone was hung up on V.

V hung up the phone on his end. He had a sense of dread about him, and now he was starting to, for the first time in his life, experience a little fear.

"Wow. I guess Moms and Terri will be *happy* that 'Victor' came to church, but they sure won't be happy when he *leaves*."

V gathered up his tapes and put them in his "secret" place.

"I can't *believe* that motherfucker just *threatened* me! What's worse than that is I can't believe I'm a little *scared*."

* * *

"Shit, girl, what you trying to do, kill me?" Junior asked.

"Naw, hon. Just tell me you *don't* like what I'm giving you," Pat said.

"I can't tell you *that*. You keep *this* up and you'll be having me fixing *you* breakfast . . . forever!"

"That's the plan. Ha ha!"

"You're crazy, girl!"

"I know. About *you*."

Junior couldn't help but look Patricia deep in her eyes and smile. The one thing he truly hoped was that she was not playing with his emotions because he had never felt this way about another person in his life.

"Besides," Pat continued, "I *know* you, and you're about to get *real* busy on this case. Am I *right*?"

"You're right."

"That phone call a few minutes ago . . . that was V, am I right?"

"Right again."

"He found something. Right?"

"Three for three."

"Okay. You give me the rest of today and then hook up with your boy on tomorrow, and then I promise to give you a break. Deal?"

"No deal."

"*What?* Why *not*?"

"Because I don't *want* you to give me a break. We'll get together when the opportunity arises. Yeah, it's time to clock on, but you and I will *make* time for each other. It's important to our relationship . . . at least *I* think so. You're so special to me, and I want what we have to grow. It's *more* than sex though. But I need for you to tell me one thing: Do you feel the same way?"

"Kiss me," Pat said.

Junior gave Pat a long passionate kiss.

"Thank you," she said.

"You're welcome. Does that mean you *don't* feel the same way?"

"I didn't *say* that. I just wanted a kiss. Of *course*, I do. You're my *man*!"

"And you're my joy, and I'm not letting *anyone* steal my joy from me!"

"Aw, you say the sweetest things."

"It's easy when you're *talking* to the sweetest thing."

"Okay, Junior, you can stop laying it on so thick now. You already have me. Besides, I don't have on my high boots!"

All Junior could do was smile.

CHAPTER 28

DIVINE INTERCEPTION

"Victor Taylor? What are you doing here? I didn't expect to see you here at church! Terri, did you do something to make him come?"

"No, Moms, this was *his* idea. *I'm* just as surprised as *you* are."

Terri was all smiles, and Moms was laughing like someone turned her tickle box over. V just stood there, wanting to smile himself, but he felt the best thing he should do right now was be the typical Victor Taylor that everyone expected.

"Would you two stop all this shi . . . stuff? What? Is hell gonna bust open because I came to church?"

"It *might*!" The Right Reverend Stanley had just walked up on the conversation and decided to chime in.

"Reverend! How are you? Ain't this a *miracle*?" Moms asked.

"Well, I wouldn't go *that* far. It's pretty amazing, I will admit. I'm glad you came, Victor."

"Yeah, well, I was sort of *motivated* into being here today," V responded.

"Some sort of *divine intervention*?" the reverend asked.

"I don't know about divine, but I *had* to be here. I've got to leave early though," he said to Terri.

"You've got to *leave*? You're going to miss my *sermon*, son!"

"Sorry about that, Rev. I guess you're gonna have to be thankful that I at least *came*, huh? I guess I'm going to have to catch the DVD."

"I guess so. Well, I've got to go and prepare for the services. Great to see you, son! Oh, and, Ms. Taylor? I apologize for my actions *and* my statements on last month. No hard feelings?"

"None, Pastor. We all learn things, right?"

"Yes, ma'am, we do. Ya'll enjoy the service, okay?"

"You too. Have a good service. Let's go grab a seat, Victor," Moms said.

"What about me, Moms?" Terri asked.

"I meant you too, dear. Sorry. I just *said* Victor, that's all."

"I know, Moms. Just playing with you."

"Oh, *you*," Moms said while hugging her daughter-in-law.

They sat down just a few minutes before the deacons got up to open the service with devotion. Scripture. Prayer. Song. Then they turned it over to the choir who led everyone into a two-minute fellowship, where people would leave their seats and go greet a member, friend, visitor, or even Victor Taylor. V never moved as people walked all over the church saying "hi" and "good to see ya" to people they came to. He did shake everyone's hand that offered it, but he didn't say a word. He just nodded. When that was over, everyone took their seats, and the church clerk got up to give the announcements. The pastor was still in his study, and one of the assistant ministers got up to do the altar call. Just as he started in on the prayer, Marco and Alphonso walked up to the row that V was sitting on and gestured for him to come out. Moms saw them.

"Victor! You can't go yet! They're praying, and no one is supposed to move during the altar call!" Moms whispered.

V looked back at the twins, and Alphonso pointed at his watch, and Marco started to come down the row to grab V, but V held up his hand to him and looked back at Moms.

"Sorry, Moms. I gotta go now. Tell the pastor sorry for me." He kissed Moms on the cheek and then kissed Terri on the lips and walked down the row, walked down the wall, and then walked up to one of the ushers on the door. This particular usher was rather large, about six feet six inches and weighing in at about 320 pounds.

"You can't leave out yet. They're still praying," the usher said.

"Say, youse better get the fuck out of the way, unlessen youse wants to get hurt," Alphonso said.

"What did you say to me, punk? Just 'cause we're in the house of the Lord don't mean I won't do what I *have* to do!" the usher responded.

No other words were spoken. Marco and Alphonso both jumped him. The other male ushers ran over to help, but once they saw how their cohort in the usher ministry was being manhandled by these two bruisers, all they could do was stand around and look. The muscle broke his arm and left him in a heap as they walked proudly out of the church, with V in tow, no less. By this time, many people toward the back of the church had stopped praying and were trying to get a better look at what had happened. The commotion had heads rising out of prayer like the wave at a football game. The preacher never raised his head in spite of all that happened.

"I *told* you we need some security at this church," a lady said to her husband sitting in the back.

"So let me get this straight," V said to the muscle while getting in the backseat of the car they drove. "You two and *I* are on the same team, right?"

Alphonso said, "Right."

"Good."

* * *

Belinda Jett was on the phone with her parents. A random conversation pursues.

"Hey, Mama! I'm fine! How are you . . . ? And Daddy . . . ? And Zeus . . . ? I know you don't like Zeus like *I* like him, but I'm still concerned. I *know* he's my dog. I love him *too*, you know . . . ? Yeah, it's not as bad as I thought it would be . . . When am I coming home? Sheesh, Mama, I *just* got here! Anyway, I got the job with the Taylor firm. Yayyy . . . ! No! Mr. Taylor is a lot nicer than what I've heard. He's handsome too . . . No, Mother, I am *not* falling for Mr. Taylor. Can't I say that a man looks good without you thinking we're having an affair? Besides, I *have* a boyfriend . . . Yes, *Samuel* . . . Okay . . . All right, Mama, but you're wrong about him . . . I just *know*, that's how. Let me ask *you* a question. Are you happy *for* me and *with* me . . . ? Thanks, Mama. Can I speak to Daddy . . . ? He's doing *what* . . . ? Mama, you need to give that man a break. He's *always* doing for you . . . How do *you* know that's what he likes to do . . . ? You better be careful. All work and no play makes Jack go out and play with someone else . . . I know, I know, I've always said that just *thinking* about you and Daddy *that* way disgusts me, but I've got to be realistic about life. You guys are married, and if Daddy is still with you, he must like *some* things about you . . . Okay, he likes *a lot* of things about you. I'm just saying . . . No,

I'm not trying . . . Okay, Mama, you know your husband. You will find out, however, that your daughter may be a little wiser than you want to believe . . . Ha ha ha! You are a funny lady! So Daddy *can't* talk . . . ? Okay, I'll wait . . .

"Hey, Daddy! How's it going . . . ? Oh, another honey-do list? Daddy . . . are you *happy* . . . ? Ecstatic? *Really* . . . ? Okay. I just asked, that's all . . . No, Mama didn't say she wasn't happy. Boy, you guys are something else. So did Mama tell you the good news . . . ? Well, thank you . . . When am I coming home? Soon, Daddy, okay? Well, look, it's getting late, and I've got a big week coming up . . . Yes, I *am* saying that I am getting off the phone. I need to get some sleep. You do want me to do *well*, don't you . . . ? That's *sweet* of you to say, Daddy . . . I love you too. Tell Mama I love her. And kiss Zeus for me . . . I *knew* you weren't going to. Talk to you guys later. Bye."

CHAPTER 29

ROI

Victor was looking over his face in the mirror in his cell. He had just shaved, and he felt better about himself. Big Percy was able to get him a razor, even though razors were not allowed in prison. After shaving, he gave the razor back to Percy. He was already in jail for no reason, and he didn't want anything *else* to hamper him getting out. He had tried to convince everyone in prison he was <u>not</u> who they *thought* he was. He could see *that* was going nowhere. Two and a half weeks in solitary made him think that his arrogance, even though he saw it as confidence, didn't amount to a hill of beans. Might as well play along, since there was nothing else he could do. Play along and plan.

Okay, I'll pretend to be V . . . for now. It might be the only thing that'll help me get out. If I keep insisting on being someone else, I might wind up with a straitjacket on! he thought.

"Feel better, sweetie?" Big Percy asked.

"Yeah, I do. Thanks for hooking me up. So you're *gay*, huh?" Victor inquired.

"That's *funny*. You already *know* this. Did your brother hit you *that* hard?"

"Yeah, I *guess* so. Say, can you do me *another* favor?"

Percy tilted his head to one side, knowing that "V" doesn't usually ask favors, and this is the second one.

"What *is* it, hon?"

"Could you stop calling me those goddamn names of endearment before I get pissed off and fuck you up!"

"*Well!* I guess you didn't forget *everything*! Anything you *say*, sir."

Victor smiled a smile of relief. He was beginning to think his brother *liked* this kind of treatment and was glad to know his brother didn't swing that way. He also saw that V had some respect in here, looking at the size of Big Percy. So now it was time to start working on a plan to get out of this hellhole.

"So do you think you can make a phone call to someone?" asked Victor.

"It *depends*."

"Depends on *what*?"

"*Two* things: *One* is who is working on guard. The *other* is what's in it for *me*."

"What do you *want*? If it's *ass*, forget it."

"It's *not* ass. Besides, I would *give* it, not *take* it. Anyway, I'm pretty sure you can't give me *freedom*. But if you could help me help my mother, *that* would be all *I* need."

"What? *Money?*"

"Well *yeah*. But you don't *have* any money, do you, V?"

A big grin broke out on Victor's face.

"You would be *surprised* at what *I* have. And besides, who said I couldn't help get you freedom? You make a phone call for me and *I'll* make sure your mama will be well taken care of. Maybe even work on that 'freedom' thing."

"Okay. So why not make your *own* phone calls?"

"That Cooper guy told me that it would be a cold day in hell before V . . . I mean, *I* would *ever* use a phone again. I sorta believe him. It's okay though. You do this for me, and your mother will never worry about money again!"

"I have one more question for you. What if I can arrange for you to make that phone call on your own?" Percy asked.

"Hell, you do *that*, and then you watch what I'll try to do for you."

* * *

V's phone rang just as his "ride" pulled up to Sabino's warehouse.

"Hello . . . ? Say, look, I can't talk right now. Let me get back at you." With that, he hung up the phone. He had looked and noticed it was Junior calling, but he knew not to say his name with Marco and Alphonso all ears. They got out of the vehicle and went inside the building. When they got inside, V was escorted to Sabino's office, where he saw Mr. Sabino, the warden, and surprisingly, Cooper. Once V was seated with the rest, Sabino made a phone call and put it on speaker. V had met the Marco and Alphonso, he knew the warden, and everybody in town knew Sabino. The only one he knew *personally* was Cooper, but he couldn't let on to that.

"Yeah!" a rough voice answered.

"Colonel? Sabino here."

"Did you get everyone assembled?"

"Yeah, they're all here. I think some of them are surprised to see one another."

"I'll bet," the colonel replied. "Gentlemen. You know *why* I've called you here, don't you?"

No one answered.

"*Hello? Answer* me, damnit!"

Cooper gulped. "Uh . . . it's *time*, sir?"

"Damn *straight*, it's time! How many of you are ready to be rich beyond your wildest dreams?"

V spoke up.

"Mr. Colonel, sir, I don't know about the rest of these jokers, but *I* am!"

"Watch your mouth, boy!" Sabino said.

"Sorry, Mr. Sabino. Not my intention to disrespect. Just answering the colonel's question."

"And I appreciate that," said the colonel. "How about *the* rest of you pansies?"

"What do *you* think, sir?" replied Sabino.

"So now *your* ass wants to get smart! Man, if you weren't a centrifugal force in this matter, I would kick your ass to the curb! But again, since I can't pull this off *without* you, I guess I'm gonna have to let that slide," the colonel said.

"So what do we do now?" asked the warden.

"Warden? Is that you?"

"Yeah, Colonel, it's me."

"Question: Did you take care of what you were assigned?"

"Everyone's lined up, sir. I had to call on a couple of favors, but I'll take care of them when I get mine."

"Good! Sabino? Has your crew perfected the mixture?"

"Tested it this week. We're a go!"

"Hot *damn*! Sounds *good*! So we ship this week, right?" The colonel was excited.

"Yes, sir, starting tomorrow morning."

"Excuse me, sir. I don't want to sound clueless, but what assignment did . . . What's your name again?" V asked.

"Cooper. That's all you need to know," Cooper replied.

"Yes . . . Mr. Cooper. That's right. We met at the prison entrance. Yeah! I remember your ugly ass. Anyway, what was *this* chicken shit supposed to do? And what the hell happened to your *face* anyway?"

"*Fuck* you, boy!" Cooper shot back.

The colonel interjected, "Calm *down*, Cooper! Well, you're a bit *nosy*, Mr. Taylor, but I'll tell you anyway. You, Marco, Alphonso, and Mr. Cooper took care of our financial front. Postage, materials we didn't have . . . you know, shit like that. You know as well as anyone that it takes money to make money, and the return on you guys' investment will extend beyond reality. Of course, *you* gave more, Mr. Taylor, so you should expect more *back*. Everyone's aware of their input and their outcomes."

"Okay, it was just that I met this guy once at the prison, and he didn't seem like the type that should be a *part* of this group. Nothing personal," he said to Cooper.

"That's how *I* take it. I'm really not afraid of you, you know," Cooper responded, scowling.

"Boys, boys . . . play nice now. We're all in this together, and this is jumping off soon. When this is all over, you'll never have to see each other again. Now if the information and finances you gave to Mr. Sabino is correct, then you should receive your 'dividends' shortly after that. Don't spend it all in one place. Hell, you couldn't if you *wanted* to! Ha ha!"

"Sounds *big*," V said.

"*Big!* This might sound funny, but *big* is too *small* a word for what's about to happen. When you literally break the banks, your lives will change *forever*!"

CHAPTER 30

THE HEART KNOWS

V was dropped off by "the punishers" in front of "his" mansion. Yes, Marco and Alphonso were the same ones that beat up and then worked for Big Daddy Thomas.

"Thanks for the ride, guys. Here's to filthy richness," V said. They didn't respond. They just sped off. V went to the black box, punched a code that he had found in the office, and the gates gave him passage to the inside of Victor's compound. Since he couldn't just talk to the box because he wasn't in a vehicle, he had to use the code. It was March, but the wind still had a little bite to it. As he walked up the long driveway, he noticed how gray everything still was, except for the grass, and this still puzzled him, but that the plants seemed to be budding, making a way for the next season.

"That's it, fellas," V spoke to the flora, "it's time for a change. As a matter of fact, it's gonna be *my* season too!"

V thought about calling up to the house and having Terri come pick him up but decided the walk would do him good. He had lost focus on the main reason for being out of jail in the first place: to prove his innocence and to get his life back. It's almost like having time off from a job and trying to give leave back to go back to work. Hard! Right now, V was having it pretty easy. But he knew he had to get to the bottom of this new situation. He still had a way to go before he reached the house, so he thought that he may as well call Junior back. He was sure glad he grabbed his leather jacket that morning.

"Hey! Junior . . . ! Yeah, it's me. Man, you are *not* gonna believe the shit that's going down. You want to know what's *funny* . . . ? I can't even tell you *what* it *is* 'cause I don't really *know*!"

"Didn't you say something about some tapes?" Junior asked.

"Yeah, I did. But what happened today overrides *anything* said on those tapes."

"Okay, V. *Talk* to me."

V paused.

"Nah, *not* on my cell . . . I *may* have said too much already. Let's hook up."

* * *

Terri was just finishing helping Moms clean off her table. She had taken Moms home from church and wound up staying there, eating dinner and talking.

"So, Moms, *how* could you *tell*? It's so *early*!" Terri asked.

"Girl, I've been around. This ain't my *first* rodeo, and it ain't new to me, you know."

"So what do you think I should *do*? He ain't gonna be happy, you know that, right?"

"Who gives a da . . . I mean, who *cares* if he's happy or not? He *will* be happy! *I'm happy!* Are you *kidding* me? I'm getting me a *grandchild*!" Moms was giddy. It was like Terri didn't hear what Moms just said.

"How do you *know* he'll be happy? He's *never* wanted this. Things are going *too* good right now for me to mess them up. Do you *really* think I should tell him? I mean, *really*, a *baby*?"

"*Look*, Terri, there are things *both* of you need to discuss with each other. There are things going on right now in *his* life that he's not divulging to you."

"Like what?" Terri asked.

"Never mind. He's a *man*, and I'm going to *let* him be a man about the whole thing."

"Moms, did Victor tell you something that he's not telling me?"

"No, *Victor* didn't. I'm just saying that I'm *sure* that the man you're with is holding back some *pertinent* information, that's all."

"Moms? *What* do you know?"

"I don't know *nothing*. I *suspect*. But I don't know."

"And what do you *suspect*?"

"Lord, have mercy! Who would've thought that when someone got pregnant, that they would become so *nosy*?"

Terri laughed and blushed all at the same time.

"Okay, Moms, you may be right. But can you at *least* give me a clue?"

"I'll tell you this *one* thing, and you'll have to figure it out from here: Don't believe everything you *see* and only *half* of what you *hear*. Got that?"

"I heard you, but I'm not quite sure what that means."

"Not yet," Moms said.

"Okay. Not yet."

"I know I said *one* thing, but I'll tell you *another* thing. Don't hold back this information from him. He *deserves* to know, and whatever his reaction is, you . . . and he will have to *deal* with it. This is *not* the end of the world, baby. It's the beginning of a new life. And right now, while there is *love* between the two of you, you *need* to take advantage of the situation. It *could* change, and things could go back to the way they *used* to be. If *that* happens, *then* what will you do? *Abort* the child? *Leave* him? No, sweetie, *now* is the time to talk about this with honesty. Let him *know* you are carrying his *child*."

Terri thought for a minute. "You *know*, Moms. You're *right*. Things have *never* been better between Victor and me. He is the man I *thought* I wanted to marry years ago, and I am loving on him more than ever. He's attentive, caring, protective, and loving. He most *definitely* needs to know. I'll tell him as *soon* as I get home. As a matter of fact . . . are you good here?"

"Am I *good* here? Girl, this is *my* home. I *better* be good here! You go on home and be with this 'mystery man' you speak of. It *surely* can't be Victor!"

"That's funny, Moms, I had thought that *very* same thing. So what are *you* trying to say? That Victor ain't *Victor*? If *that's* true, who *is* he then?"

Moms got up from the seat she was in and headed for the door.

"You didn't hear me say *that*. Come on, Terri. You'd better get home before it gets too late."

"Moms? You didn't *answer* me. *You* would *know*. Is that Victor I'm loving on, or is that someone else? All I ask from you is the truth."

Moms turned around at the door to find Terri in her face.

"Terri . . . that *is* my son . . . and *that*, my dear, *is* the truth."

Moms hugged Terri, who started to tear up, and helped her with her coat. She kissed Terri on the cheek and then opened the front door.

"Terri, sometimes, in life, we'll find ourselves at a crossroads, and we know that we have to go down *one* way or another. I can't tell you which road to take, but whatever road you take, make sure that your *heart* is leading you, along *with* your *head*. Everyone on the outside wants to tell you how to conduct yourself or how to live your life. But in the end, *your* happiness will not be determined by what *others* see but rather the choices you make about your *own* life. If you trust your heart, you'll figure this out. By the way, tell *Victor* I said hi. And you take care of yourself. Wow. A *grandchild*!"

Terri walked out of Moms's house with a tear running down her face. She never looked back; she just climbed into her vehicle and headed home. At this point, she didn't know what to think.

CHAPTER 31

I'M LISTENING

When V reached the house, he noticed that no one was there. The alarm was still set, and after disarming it, he went in and headed straight to the office. He didn't even close the door behind him. He called Junior back on a secure line in the office. They were planning.

"So while you were there, did you see—"

"Hold on, man. Let me plug up my cell. Battery's about dead." V plugged up his cell and picked up the receiver in the office.

"Okay, Junior. I'm back."

"Cool. Did you see anything suspicious?" Junior asked.

"Naw, man. I saw workers packing boxes, but what they were putting in the boxes looked harmless."

"What did it *look* like were going into the boxes?"

"From what I could *see*, they looked like gears. You know, like the kind that you find on bicycles? No more than about three to a box. The boxes weren't that big."

"Damn. That doesn't help me at all. Nothing *else* suspicious, other than your *meeting*, that is?"

"No. Shit, man! I'm sorry, dude, but I'm holding back on you . . . not on *purpose* though, dawg. I just forgot."

"What is it?"

"They handed everyone a parting gift. It's packed in one of the little boxes they had. I was gonna check it out first and *then* get back at you."

"*Motherfucker*. What's in it?"

"I don't know. Hadn't opened it yet? Let me call you back after I check it out, okay?"

"Aw-ight, cool."

145

"Oh, and, Junior?"

"Yeah, dude."

"Sorry about that, aw-ight?"

"We cool, man. No prob. Get back at ya, boy."

"Later."

V hung up and grabbed a paper cutter and opened up the box he had brought in. The office door wasn't closed all the way, and Terri entered before he could take out the contents.

"Who was that on the *phone*, Victor?"

"*Terri?* When did *you* get here? I didn't know—"

"Yeah, yeah, you didn't know I was home. Who was that on the *phone*, Victor? You seemed quite *friendly* to him or her, *whoever* it was. Did I hear you say *Junior?*"

V had to think and react fast.

"Wait just a *damn* minute! You sneak up on me, *eavesdrop* on *my* conversation, and then question *who* I talk to and *how* I talk to them in my *own* goddamn *house*? You *know* I'm not gonna have *this*! Why are you *attacking* me anyway?"

"Hell, *I* don't know. Maybe my *hormones* are acting up. But *you* need to cut the *shit*, Victor! That is, if that is who you *are*. Now you haven't behaved this way in *weeks*, and all of a *sudden*, you want to go *off* on me? *Hell* no! I'm not *buying* it. But you *need* to sit there and *listen* to me because I have something to *tell* you, and then after you *hear* it, let's *see* what the *hell* you have to *say*. I'm *pregnant*. It's *yours*. *Now* what?" she said, a tear forming in her eye.

V just sat in the chair, staring at her, speechless. His Samsung rang. And rang. And rang. V finally woke out of his stupor. He answered but didn't even look to see who it was.

"Victor Taylor. It's my time, but it's your dime."

"Well, I'll be *damned*! I thought that was *my* line!"

V pulled the phone away from his ear, covered the speaker with his hand, and looked at Terri.

"Terri, can I take this call in private? I'll talk with you as *soon* as this is over. *Okay?*"

"Sure." Terri turned to leave the room.

"Oh, Terri," V called out to her. "I'm sorry."

Terri just looked at him emotionless and closed the door behind her as she left. V just closed his eyes and tried to compose himself. He returned to his call.

"Vincent! Now how were *you* able to make a phone call?" V asked.

"Damn, you *have* gotten smarter! Don't worry, just like *your* call to Moms wasn't recorded, this one isn't either. And if you have the office door closed *completely, that* room is soundproof, so I'm not worried about anyone hearing you in there. But I have *my* ways, just like you have *your* ways," Victor said to V.

"But you're not *me*. How are you able to make the moves in prison that I did?"

"You know what? I was wrong. You *are* stupid. I <u>am</u> you in *prison*, you *dick*! I can *do* what you could do, but I can do *more*. Tell me, what the *fuck* are you doing about getting me, I mean, *you* out of this hellhole?"

V was speechless. He really hadn't tried as hard as he could have. Things were *too* good.

Victor continued. "So I guess you thought you'd just let me receive *your* death sentence and you could just go on being me without a care in the world, right? Ha! Hell, *even* if they didn't kill me, at *least* I'd never get out, *right*? You got me good . . . I'll give you that. But you don't really know me at *all*, do you? *Boy*, just like you got *yourself* out of here, I'm going to get *myself* out of here too."

"How do you propose to do that?" V asked.

"Actually, the same damn way *you* did. By using my *head*! Not the *exact* same way you did, mind you. No, but by using my 'famous attorney brother,' Mr. Victor Taylor, *that's* how."

"You tell me why I should help you. The way you treated me and everyone else, as a matter of fact, is enough for me to let your ass *die* in prison!"

"Yeah, that would *sound* right if it came from *me*! But, Vincent, my dear brother, that is *not* in your nature. You are *not* the cold-blooded bastard that cares less about others. No. You *care*. You *say* you're innocent of murder, but then you turn around and *allow* a *killing*? And besides, could you *really* live with yourself knowing that you let your own *name* be tainted for the rest of your life? And you love *Moms*, right? What would *she* think if she knew you did *nothing* to help your *only* brother get out of prison and *off* death row *if* you had the power to do so? *Especially* when she finds out that you are who you *really* are. You *know* how she feels about her *precious* Vincent. Would that *matter* to you at *all*? What about *Cassie*? Couldn't be with *her* anymore, *could* you? What about *Terri*? Your *new* wife. Do you think *she'll* want to stay with you when she finds out that you're *just* as cold as you say *I* am? You *know* that bitch wants a *baby*, don't you?"

"Wait just a *damn* minute, brother! Terri is no *bitch*! She's a *fine* lady and deserves the best. She only wanted the best for and from you, but tell me, Vic, what did you want from *her*?"

"*That's* none of your goddamn business . . . but I can *see* that you have grown fond of her, am I *right*? Hell, you can *have* that heifer. She's *worrisome*."

V didn't respond. Not only did he know that his brother spoke the truth about his feelings for Terri, but he was also stunned at how Victor felt about her.

Victor continued. "That's okay. Your silence tells it all. Now *this* is what you are going to do. It *will* free me from prison and clear your name at the same time. The question to you *now* is, are you interested or not?"

"I am. But why all of a sudden are you willing to help me? Could it be that something big is about to go down and you could benefit from it?" Victor hesitated for a second but then responded.

"What do you *know*, V?"

"I don't know shit, Vic."

"You're lying."

"No, I'm not. I'm *listening*. What's your plan?"

CHAPTER 32

LET'S GET SERIOUS

"What the *fuck*?" Cooper blasted in the warden's office, going off.

"*Cooper?* Close the *door*! What's *wrong*?"

Cooper slammed the door behind him. "How the *fuck* was that Vincent Taylor able to make a *phone call*? *Damnit*, it's like he can do any *goddamned* thing he *wants* to! I can't *touch* him! I can't touch *Casey*! Damnit, when do *I* get to have some restitution? When do I have *my* day?"

"You'll have your day when all this shit is *over, that's* when. What you *need* to do is go somewhere and sit your ass down until it's through. Do you need some time off?"

"Hell naw. My wife would be asking me questions and shit as to *why* I'm off and having me do all kinds of *honey-do* shit. You already know I'm not a very good liar, so when my wife starts in on me, I *might* fuck up."

"I don't know," the warden replied. "You've been doing pretty well with the lying so far, don't you think?"

Cooper couldn't respond. He just looked at the warden, smiled, and then left.

* * *

Patricia just stepped out of the shower and wrapped a towel around her as she came into the room where Junior was sitting.

"Were you just on the phone?" she asked.

"Yeah. That was V. He's supposed to get back at me. Damn, girl, you know I can't concentrate when you walk around like that! That turns me the hell *on!*"

"What? Me in a *towel?* Or the fact you know what's *underneath?*" she teased.

"*Both.* Pat, baby, we're supposed to be *working.* I love you. More than *anything* or *anyone* I ever have before. But if we keep on sexing each other *every single chance* we get, we won't finish the task at hand. I know most guys wouldn't think like me. They would be glad to get it in and sometimes beg for it whenever they could. We're good together, and I love the deepness of our love for each other. But we need to work *now* so we can play *later.*"

"Okay, baby. I'll go and put on some clothes," she said while leaving the room.

"You're not *mad,* are you, Pat? You understand, *right?*"

Pat walked back toward Junior and kissed him lightly on the lips.

"No, I'm not mad at all, and I really *do* understand. You're right, and I respect your professionalism. You are the *man,* and I am your woman. Let's get to work, baby."

Pat left to go put on some clothes. Junior was left alone with his thoughts until she returned. *Damn, dude. That is the sweetest woman you've ever met, and you're having the best relationship you've ever had. Don't blow it with her over some bullshit job. Better yet, let's get this shit over with.*

CHAPTER 33

MEETING UP

Tuesday had come, and Terri and V *still* hadn't talked yet about the new circumstance in their lives. This was totally new for the both of them, and V felt a sense of misdirection. He thought this situation was just about over, so hearing about a baby shook things up for him. He made it a point to avoid Terri at all costs, and Terri could sense that he was just as terrified as she was, so Terri thought she'd go and do some shopping for herself, maybe for the baby. She wasn't that far along as to be showing, but her moods were starting to be affected. She was easily emotional at the slightest things: the toaster cooking her bread darker than she wanted, the ice cream melting before she finished it, a commercial about kittens, a GEICO commercial. She was on an emotional rollercoaster. Shopping should do the trick for now, hopefully. She decided to go to Macy's and make a few purchases. She didn't need anything, so this was a form of therapy for her. She had money, so that was never an issue, but Terri had always been frugal, so she shopped in the clearance areas. Discounts, baby! She had heard it said that the rich are rich because they save more than they spend. Amazing how we all would be better off if we could follow that rule.

"Hey, Terri!"

Terri turned around to be in the presence of Cassie.

"Cassie? How are you?"

"I'm good, and you?"

"Couldn't be better!" Terri said.

"So you're shopping, I see? For anyone in particular?"

You're a nosy heifer, Terri thought.

"Well, next Saturday is Victor's birthday. But you already knew that, didn't you, seeing how Victor and Vincent are twins, and Vincent is your *boyfriend*. I'm just shopping though. Maybe something for me. Maybe something for Victor. Maybe something for the baby."

"The *baby*? Your *baby*? *You're pregnant?*" Cassie asked.

Terri questioned herself as to *why the hell* did she just divulge that information to Cassie.

"Yes, I am!"

"It's *Victor's?*"

"What?" Terri responded, almost too loudly.

"I mean, does he *know?*"

"Yes, *he* knows. I don't know how he *feels* about it yet. I just told him a couple of days ago, and we haven't talked about it."

Terri felt like she probably shouldn't have told Cassie that bit of information either. She just got caught up in the conversation.

"*Wow*. I don't know what to *say*."

"Well, how about *congratulations?* 'I'm *happy* for you.' *Anything* like that would probably be appropriate."

"Yeah, I'm sorry. You're right. *Congratulations*, girl. I hope *everything* works out for you and Victor."

"Well, thank you, Cassie."

"Say, Terri, look, I'm supposed to be somewhere. I just saw you and thought I'd say hi."

"Oh okay . . . hi. Good to see you."

"Yeah, you too. I'll see you around."

"Okay."

Hell, not if I see you first . . . bitch!

As Cassie rushed off, Terri suddenly remembered what Moms said to her. "Don't believe everything you *see* and only *half* of what you *hear*." For some reason, this saying started to come to life when it came to Cassie.

"You know *what*, Cassie?" Terri said to herself, "I just don't *trust* your ass."

* * *

"A piggy bank? That's *all* that was in this box?" Junior asked. He and Patricia met up with V at Victor's office, and they were in a private conference room. It was Wednesday, March 9.

"That's it. Could it mean something else?" V asked.

"Was there any money in it?" Pat asked.

"Nope. I shook it real good," V answered.

"Well, *hell*, this case is going nowhere. Pat or I have to get inside that plant and see if we can come across some clues," Junior said.

"Dude, why do you think your case has anything to do with Sabino and his plant anyway?" V asked.

"I have my source, and Pat has her intuitions. Can't divulge *everything*. You understand, right?"

"Aw, man, I thought we were boys! You can't tell your best homey?"

"Nope."

"I *knew* you couldn't. I was just playing."

"He's cute. Are you sure Victor is *not* as cute?" Pat asked.

"He's only cute because he *looks* like me, but I don't think you were talking about looks, am I *right*?" V asked.

"Damn, and he could be an agent as *well*! *So* perceptive! But yeah, you're not bad-looking either. Ha ha!"

"Come on, Pat. V has feelings too. You're trying to be funny."

"It's okay," V said. "She's not hurting me. She has *your* sense of humor, so I'm used to it."

Pat and Junior looked at each other and smiled. They almost forgot they were in a conference room at a high-end, high-class, and high-priced law firm.

"Stop all that lovey-dovey shit! Would you guys like something to drink?"

"Sure. What you *got*?" Junior asked.

"What you *want*?"

"Aww shit! You got it like *that*? Let me *ask* you something, V. Are you *sure* you want to give all this up to get that . . . to get Victor out of prison?"

V gave a sly look over his shoulder. "Who *said* I was giving all this up?"

"*Uh* oh. One *more* question: Do you need my *help*?"

"Not right now. But I *might*. If I do, are you *down*?"

"Like the opposite of *up*, bro!"

"Cool! Excuse me." V pushed on an intercom. "Hello, Ms. Jett? This is Victor Taylor. I know that you don't usually do gofer work for me, but would you *indulge* me this once?"

"Yes, sir, what do you need?"

"I am in conference room no. 3. Could you bring some lemonade?" V looked at Pat and Junior for approval. "For me and my guests. Four glasses, please. And a pitcher of water. Okay?"

"I'll be there as soon as I can, sir."

"Thank you."

"Damn, son. So I can assume that Belinda is *not* a secretary, right?" Junior said.

"Correct."

"So why *her*? And why *four* glasses? It's only *three* of us."

"Four reasons. One, she's *new* here. Two, she's *eager* to please her boss. Three, she won't question my *authority* nor my *instructions*, and I'm going to need her to write up some important documents for me. And four, it won't be three once she joins us. Excuse me again." V pushed the intercom again.

"Lisa?"

"Yes, Mr. Taylor?"

"*Where* is Chase?"

"He's in court, sir. From what I hear, he's *killing* the case and will probably be finished today!"

"You seem to be a little more excited than you *should* be about a case that you probably *shouldn't* know anything about. Is something going on that I need to *know* about?"

"Uh . . . sir . . . uh, Chase and I . . . well . . . we're *seeing* each other. Is that a *problem*?"

V smiled, thinking he would have some fun.

"You *do* know that you should have told me when it *started*, don't you?"

"Yes, sir. I apologize."

"Two wrongs do not make a right, Lisa."

"I know, sir. But three rights make a left, correct?"

Pat and Junior laughed in the background, and all V could do was blush and smile.

"Yes. That *is* correct. Could you have Mr. Morton contact me ASAP? *Extremely* important and could be quite a boost in his paycheck . . . or should I say in *yours*?"

"Mr. *Taylor*! I'll tell him."

"Thank you. I expect him to contact me promptly."

V got off the intercom just as there was a knock on the conference room door. He went over to open it, and Belinda Jett entered the room carrying a tray with the requested items on it.

"Here you are, Mr. Taylor. Where do you want me to place it?"

"Over here where we're sitting. I need to speak with you while you're here. Do you have a minute?"

"Yes, sir. What can I do for you?"

CHAPTER 34

WHAT'S LOVE GOT TO DO WITH IT ANYWAY?

This particular restaurant was dark on the inside, even in the daytime. People like to call it ambiance, but it was just dark. Wooden tables that had been carved on by patrons was one of the little advertising gimmicks it used to get people to come there. One could eat there and "leave your autograph right on the table." The food was great, and the service deserved a good tip. The only problem was that it was off the beaten path, and it took more than a notion to go there. If you wanted discretion, go here. The name of the place? Elaine's.

"Yeah, that's great information! You have *more* than honored your requirements, so have no fear that I will honor my promises to you. Have a great day, my friend."

The colonel had just gotten off the phone with an informant that kept him abreast and fed him new information when it occurred. The last bit of info had the colonel smiling. He was getting ready to get up and leave the restaurant where he was eating when his phone rang.

"Yeah."

"Colonel? Sabino. Hey, would it be a problem if things happened sooner than promised?"

"Hell no! No problem at all. What's going on?"

"Well, it looks like things could be in *full* swing by next Saturday."

"Shit, kick it off then! It's all fine by me. The only thing I ask from you is a seventy-two-hour window so I can make my final arrangements. Can you do that for me?" the colonel asked.

"Well, from all that you are doing for the rest of us, I believe I can handle that little bit. Just wanted to let you know that things are in place and to see if it would be okay for it to be bumped up."

"Sabino, you have been a part of this since the beginning and have proven yourself to be of *great* worth. I will not forget it, and I *promise* you, neither will you."

"Okay. I'll get back with you when it's time."

"All right. Bye."

The colonel hung up, got up from the table, put on his coat and hat that came down over his face, and headed out of the restaurant. Junior and Pat were headed in at the same time, and they almost knocked each other down.

"Excuse me," said Junior.

"No, excuse me," replied the colonel.

The waitress came to seat Pat and Junior. When they were seated, Junior noticed that Pat had a strange look on her face.

"What's wrong, Patricia?"

"That man we ran into. He looked familiar, but I didn't see him *real* well. It just seemed like I *knew* him from someplace."

"Really? From *where*?"

"I can't really say. He just seemed like someone familiar, that's all."

"Maybe he's a long-lost uncle or something. Ha!"

"Maybe. But if I ever see him again, I'm sure going to ask him a few."

"Okay. So what do you think about V's news about having a baby?"

"*Wow* is all I can say. I want to be happy for him, but isn't that his *brother's* wife? Sorta messed *up*, don't you think?"

"Yeah, it is. I can't really tell if he's *happy* or *scared*. I'm happy for him though. I hope she lets him be the daddy to that baby and not just the father."

"Right. Even if they decide *not* to be a couple," Pat replied.

"So you're big on family, huh?"

"Well, when your mama takes you away from your daddy and . . ." Pat paused.

"And what? What is it, Pat?"

"I miss my daddy. That's all."

"I know, baby. How about I help you find him? I am FBI, you know."

"Oh *really*? Yeah, baby . . . That'll be nice . . . even if it *is* a shot in the dark. You know, for us *supposed* to be dealing with one particular case, we sure do have a lot of *shit* on our laps, don't we?"

"Yeah, we sure do, baby. We sure do."

* * *

V was driving down the road when his phone rang.

"You have *got* to be *kidding* me! Terri is *pregnant*? I thought you said you didn't *want* any children! And now she's *pregnant*? I'll be *damned*! That's all I can say right now. I thought you were using protection! *Shit*, Victor! *Terri* is pregnant! And it's yours, right? Damn!"

Cassie was giving V an earful through the speakers of his cell phone. Of course, she thought it was *Victor* she was berating, but that didn't matter to V at the moment. In all reality, *his* girlfriend was mad at his *brother* for getting his *own* wife pregnant. To make matters worse, his brother's *wife* was having a baby that belonged to *V*.

"You know, you told me that it was going to be you and me—not you, she, and baby makes three! So where do *I* fit in this picture *now*, Vic? *Huh*? Can you *tell* me that? What do *I* do now? Be the damn *godmother*? When's the last time you sexed *me*, motherfucker? I would have gladly had a baby with you, but then you always said you didn't want no babies! We had *plans*, Victor! Now how does *this* change our plans? Huh? Say *something*, shit!"

V had had enough. He pulled over to the side of the road to make sure he was clear about what he would say.

"You know *what*?" V asked. "I've been thinking about you and your trifling ways here lately anyway. You didn't love my brother. You *couldn't* have, not and have the relationship you had with *me*! So I thought, if that ass couldn't love someone that loved *her* so much, how in the *hell* could she love *me*, who didn't give a damn about *anyone*? And then it *hit* me: You don't love me *either*. But you love what I can *do* for you, right? You love the *money*, don't you? And with what was promised you financially, you could put up with some shit, *couldn't* you? See, girls like you want a *contract* when guys like V want a relationship. They can't get with you unless they come with some type of financial assistance first. And then it has to be consistent for someone like you to think you're paying them back by giving up the pussy. You *think* about that the *next* time a man wants to have something serious with you. If he's for *real*, you won't have to *worry* if he'll come through for you with a little help now and then. But hey, now I have the tapes, so I have enough proof on your ass that you won't cause me any trouble. As far as you and I are concerned, *fuck you*! We are no *more*! Go back to your Vincent and see how far you get. Or better yet, should I say your *Roger*? See, I'm not stupid, bitch, but I am pissed! But know this as well: Victor Taylor is not completely heartless. I'm not going to leave you without hooking you up. I will give you one fourth of what I promised. Take it or leave it and I need my answer right *now*!"

"Wait a minute, Victor, can't we talk ab—"

"*What* the fuck did I just *say*? That's 1.25 mil. *Take* it or *leave* it or the decision will be made *for* you and you *won't* like it!"

There was a bit of silence and then . . .

"Okay . . . I'll take it."

"Good. Bye . . . hoe!"

V hung up the phone and just looked at it. He couldn't believe he did what he just did, but he felt it was the right thing. He *knew* it hurt Cassie to be dumped the way she was, but it hurt him too because he not only dumped Cassie for Victor, but for himself as well. He couldn't control the one single tear that ran down his face. He couldn't deny that he loved Terri, but he would miss Cassie, as if she had just died. At one time, he thought he was going to ask her to marry him. He felt like such a fool. He just hoped that all the pain he was experiencing would be worth it in the end. He decided to call Terri. It had been a whole week, and V had been avoiding the situation about the baby.

"Hello, Terri? What you doing? Well, I'm on my way home. I'm ready to talk if you are."

CHAPTER 35

PROPER PAPERWORK AND PRODUCT

"Hello? May I speak to Kevin Casey?"
"Yeah, hold on for a minute," Debra said. "Kev? Telephone!"

Kevin came to the phone.

"Hello, Casey here."

"Officer Casey? This is the warden. I'm calling to let you know you can come back to work now. How's that sound to you?"

"Well, that sounds pretty white of you."

"What?"

"I'm sorry about that. What I *meant* to say is you can take this job and *shove* it up your *ass*! Was *that* better for you to understand?"

"Yes. Yes, it *was*. I guess you know that you won't receive any type of *referral* from me if you *need* it, right?"

"I won't need it."

"Pretty *sure* of yourself, *aren't* you? Well, what if I told you I can fix it where you don't work *anywhere* else in this town again?"

"Then I would think you to be a *petty* person, being a man of your stature. But hey, do what you feel you have to do. Whatever makes you feel better or more of a man, you *do* that. Hell, even if you have to *kill* someone to get what you want, go ahead. But then again, you can only kill so *many* people and get away with it before you get *caught*, right? Have a nice life, Warden."

With that, Kevin hung up the phone. Debra was listening.

"Kevin! That was the *warden* on the phone? Telling you to come back to *work*? You're not *working* anywhere! How could you *say* those things to him?"

"I may not be working, but that doesn't mean I'm not working on *something*. Debra, do you *love* me?"

"Yes, I *believe* I do."

"That's *funny*. Do you trust me? Because right now, I need you to. I got this, and you and I are going to be okay. *Okay? Trust* me?" he asked, reaching out to hold her.

"Okay, Kev. I trust you. We'll be okay, right?" Debra was worried, but she melted in Kevin's arms just the same.

"I promise. We'll be just fine."

* * *

Chase Morton and V were meeting in Victor Taylor's office. It was now Tuesday, March 15.

"Okay, Chase, did you prepare those forms I asked you to?"

"Yes, sir, Mr. Taylor. These papers, along with the new evidence you say you have, should be enough to get your brother out of jail."

"Good. You know, you're a great lawyer. Has anyone ever told you that?" V complimented.

"Yes, sir. One person has."

"Lisa, right?"

Chase looked up with a surprised look on his face.

"Uh yes, sir. You *know*?"

"I know. But don't worry. Just continue to keep it as hush-hush as you possibly can from everyone else and you'll be fine. By the way, thank you for all you've done for me *and* this firm. You know what, I'd bet you could run this firm, if you *had* to."

"Why, thank you, sir. I try. And will continue to try to give you my best."

"You're the best *I've* ever seen. Almost as good as *me*. Could you send in Ms. Jett when you step out? Thanks."

"Sure. And thanks again. Uh, excuse me, Mr. Taylor?"

"Yes?"

"Did you *mean* what you said about me running this firm? That has *always* been my dream. That's why I work so diligently for you. It helps to think someone like yourself believes I'm doing a good job."

"I *meant* it, Chase. You are the *best* lawyer that I have *ever* worked with. I would even venture to say that you are a *better* lawyer than I am." V chuckled inside; Chase would *never* know how true that was.

V reached out to shake Chase's hand. Chase returned the grip and smiled. Chase Morton exited, and within a few seconds, Belinda Jett entered.

"Ms. Jett. Please sit down."

"Thank you, sir."

"Are we all finished with our assignments?"

"Yes, sir! I feel you'll be very pleased with these documents."

"Okay. Well, look for a bonus on your next paycheck. Hell, who knows, maybe even a promotion."

"Thank you, sir. Uh . . . sir?"

"Yes, Ms. Jett?"

"Aren't you going to read the papers to make sure I covered all bases?"

"Nope. I trust you. Besides, if I didn't feel that you could accomplish the task placed before you, I never wouldn't have called on you. You do feel confident you did a good job, don't you?"

"No, sir."

"No?"

"No, sir. I feel confident that I did a *great* job on this assignment!"

"Now *that's* what I wanted to hear. Thank you for everything. I'll see you out."

V escorted Belinda out of "his" office and then sat back in the big leather chair behind the huge desk. He perused over the paperwork that he now had and felt a sense of accomplishment. He had all he needed to prove his innocence, except for one thing: evidence that would change everything. It just so happened that his brother Victor said that he could supply that. V could have easily gotten mad, thinking that his brother was privy to this information all along, but thought that what *he* had put into play would more than make up for anything his brother had done to him or not done *for* him. He looked at the calendar on his desk, and it hit him that he almost forgot about his and his brother's birthday that was coming up this very Saturday. *What presents we will receive on Saturday?* he thought. *Surprise!*

"Lisa? Could you get me Judge Campbell on the phone? If he's in court, tell him to call for a recess and take my call."

"Yes, sir, I can. But I have a message for you. I took it while you were in your meetings. You need to go to the conference room where you had your meetings earlier this week. The janitor found something. Sounded important."

V didn't know which action to take. *What's more important?*

"Okay, Lisa. I'll check out the conference room situation, but when you see me get off that elevator coming back, I need you to make that call. Okay?"

"Yes, sir."

V got from behind the desk and headed for the conference room. When he got there, there was red hazmat tape that had been draped around the door. The janitor who discovered the "problem" was standing outside the door, as if he were standing guard.

"What's going on, Jake?" V asked. He had been there long enough to learn a few people's names, and the four janitors were no exception.

"Mr. Taylor, when I found what I found, I didn't know what to do! I locked up the room and closed it off! You have got to see this!"

Jake took the red tape off the door and unlocked it so they could enter.

"Look over there!" Jake pointed.

Right where Pat, Junior, and V had met on Tuesday was a pile of white powdery substance. V stuck his pinkie in it and smelled it.

"I don't know if that's smart, Mr. Taylor! You don't know what that is! Could be dangerous!"

"You're right, Jake. I took a stupid chance just then. But it looked so familiar I forgot to practice safety. You don't have to worry. It's harmless old baking soda. You can go back to work now, but thanks for looking out for the safety of my people. I got this now, Jake. Go on."

"Are you sure, sir? If it's just baking soda, I could just sweep it up and trash it."

"No, that's okay. I'm here now, so I'll take responsibility for this mess. You forget this is because of me and my friends who met in this room, so I'll take care of this. Now that's final, you hear me?"

"Yes, sir. I'll continue to keep my eyes out for anything else suspicious, and I'll tell my crew to do the same."

"Thanks, Jake. See you around."

As soon as Jake had left and closed the door behind him, V went over to the door and locked it and pulled out his phone.

"Junior? Say, dude, you and Pat need to get over here to the office ASAP! I think you might want to see this!"

CHAPTER 36

WRAP UP

V was on his way home. It was later than usual, but it was only because he had just left the office from meeting with Junior and Pat. He was stoked but scared at the same time. Whoever is behind all this "boxes" and "money" situation must be a *genius*. V knew that even though Pat and Junior had some new *evidence* to stop a major drug shipment, they didn't have the time to put together a team or the necessary paperwork to put a stop to what was about to happen. The pile of powder that was found in the conference room was a *form* of drug, but it wasn't cocaine. This was Junior, Pat, and V's assessment of the situation.

"All I know is when we entered this room, there was this *stuff*," V said.

"How did it get here? Who was in here last?" Pat asked.

"Just you two and I . . . and Ms. Jett, of course."

"Where is the piggy bank?" Junior asked.

"Oh, I took that home. It's in my study."

"Well, where is the *box* it was in?" Junior inquired.

"That's just it. The powder is where the *box* was sitting. Do you remember Ms. Jett accidentally wasting the pitcher of water on the box, and we told her it was okay? I told her that someone else would clean it up, but I *forgot* to tell someone about it."

"So the water made the box break down into *this*?" asked Pat.

"Looks like it."

"Ingenious!" said Junior. "As long as it's in *box* form, you can't smell the *drug*. And it doesn't change into something you can use until it gets *wet*! When it dries, it dries into a powder! That's smart as *hell*! So, V, when you first got this box, was it covered with anything else?"

"As a matter of fact, it was! It was some sort of plastic seal. I mean, I took it off when I opened it. I'll be damned!"

Pat chimed in. "Yeah, that way, when they ship them, they *couldn't* get wet! If they were found to be suspicious and opened, they would find nothing in them but . . . what did you say, V . . . gears? They have no *smell* so a dog couldn't sniff them out. *Wow*!"

"Damn *straight*, wow! So they could ship out mass productions of these boxes *wherever* they wanted to and *no one* would be the *wiser*! So, V, this is supposed to go down *when*?"

"Well, it was supposed to go down in a couple of weeks, but I got a call yesterday telling me to prepare to break the banks this weekend! I wish I knew what the hell *that* meant!"

"Damn, today is *Thursday*! It ain't *shit* we can do to stop this movement! It appears to be too large and already in motion. They probably have already made their shipments. Damn, we could've *used* those extra weeks," Junior said.

"So what do we do with this *stuff*? We can't sell it, we can't use it, and we sure the hell can't *store* this shit," Pat asked.

"Shit, *I* don't know what to do with it! Do we *flush* it?" V asked.

"*Hell* no! Let's get it bagged up, and . . . do you have some bags, V?"

"Yep. Be right back. Don't open this door for anyone. I have a key."

Pat and Junior were left alone while V went to get some storage bags.

"Well, we *almost* broke the case open. We were so *close* too!" Pat said.

"Yeah. So what do we do now?"

"How about find my father? I *know* we can do that. We're not the best . . . yet . . . but we're pretty good together."

"We *are* pretty good together. Would you marry me?"

Pat gulped.

"What? *That* was random. Are you *serious*, Junior?"

"I don't know *where* that came from, but *yeah* . . . I'm *serious*. Would you have me as your husband? Because I sure do want you to be my wife."

"I expected a much more romantic way of asking. Here we are, getting ready to sweep up some kind of drug that we don't even know what it *does*. You ask me that *now*? Damn. Can I *think* about it?" Pat asked.

"Uh yeah. I *guess* so, if you need to."

"Okay, thanks."

There was that awkward silence when you don't really know what to say next.

"All right. I've thought about it. *Yes*, I'll marry you!" Pat said.

"*Really?* Oh, Patricia, you've made me the *happiest* man alive!"

With that, he had embraced Pat and kissed her long and hard. V walked in on them, but they never noticed. He locked the door back behind him.

"Ahem!" V said.

"Oh, V. Did you find what you were looking for?" Junior asked.

"Yes, I did. Did *you?*"

"Oh *yes!*" Junior said, looking lovingly at Pat.

"Good. Let's get this shit up and get the hell out of here! Besides, looks like you two need a damn *room!*"

CHAPTER 37

EVERYTHING IS A CHOICE

It was Friday morning, and V was in the study. He couldn't arrange an early meeting with Victor at the prison, so he would be seeing him later that evening. If you are Victor Taylor, then you can meet when you want to and make things happen after work hours. This time V was glad that it wasn't an early meeting. So he called in to the office and turned the helm over to Chase. He still had a couple of things to hash out and wasn't sure he would have the time to get them done. But one thing was for sure: He would make the attempt.

"Let me try this," he said while dialing.

"Hello, Judge Campbell? Victor Taylor here. Say, do you remember that proposition you and your benefactors keep offering? Are your people still interested . . . ? Yeah, let's just say I've had a change of mind . . . Yeah . . . Yeah . . . I already have. You sound surprised. You should know by now that if I *do* something, I'm *prepared* to do it, right . . . ? Okay then. You'll have the papers ready by this evening . . . ? Yes, sir. No, thank *you* . . . ! Am I *sure*? You know what, forget the whole thing . . . ! Of *course*, I'm joking, and I am most definitely sure of what I'm doing. I'll see you at your office *this* evening when I pick up those papers I need, and then I'll sign those other papers *you* need. I'll call when I get there . . . Good-bye."

No sooner than he hung up when his phone rang. It was Moms.

"Hello, Moms."

"Hey there, son! Can I speak to Victor?"

"Huh? This *is* Victor."

"No, it's not. Vincent, *where* is Victor?"

V became silent. He was busted.

"What the hell, Moms? What do you *mean*? You *know* this is me?"
"Oh really? Terri is pregnant, right?"
"Yeah, so what?"
"Have you moved *out* yet?"
"What? *No, Moms!*"
"Oh, so you put *Terri* out, huh?"
"No, why would I do *that*?"
"Well, did you file for *divorce* yet?"
"Naw, Moms, I didn't file for any *divorce*! Why are you asking all these questions?"
"Because *Victor* would have already done *one* of these things *or* even *worse!*"

V was stumped.

"Uh . . . okay. Hi, Moms. How long have you known?"
"Hi, Vinny. I've known for a while. Where's *Victor*?"
"In prison, but I'm getting him out today."
"*Prison?* How long has he been in prison?"
"Since your big dinner."
"Hmm. I *wondered* why you wouldn't look me in the eyes that Sunday. But I caught you once. I knew you'd get too comfortable and forget. I have a question, Vinny: How are you going to be able to get your brother out of prison?"
"Come on, Moms. Does it *matter*? I'm doing for him what he *wouldn't* do for me! He says he has evidence to clear my *name*! Isn't that great?"
"It *is*, son. Why didn't you tell Terri who you really were?"
"I *couldn't* . . . not and clear my name at the same *time*. If I had told her when I got out, I wouldn't have stayed out for long. I *know* this. She loves *Victor*."
"Are you *sure*? Maybe she *thought* she loved Victor. Think about this: If Victor behaved the way you behave, can you see or feel the genuine love she would have for him?"
"I *can*. But, Moms, I'm *not* Victor! I'm *Vincent*! Are *you* saying that she loves *me* instead of him?"
"No. *I'm* saying it!" Terri said. She walked in on the conversation, and V was so caught up he hadn't noticed.
"*Terri!* Look, Moms, I gotta go. I'll call you later."
"Bye, baby. Handle yo' business."

V just sat there looking at Terri who was looking at him.

"Terri. How *long* did *you* know?"

"Not long. Start putting two and two together. Never *did* add up to four. I remember how helpful and caring and thoughtful V used to be when I saw *him*. *Always* ready to help a friend when he could. He didn't have much, but that didn't stop him from *trying*. Victor . . . for as *long* as I've known him . . . *never* lifted a finger for anyone but himself. He had what he *called* a good friend from college who needed to borrow $100—*$100*, mind you! He just wouldn't *do* it, told the guy to get a paper route. Just *plain* evil. And you know, I thought it was the *head butt* that knocked some kindness into Victor, but there was too much of the typical Victor toward other people and the opposite toward me when we were alone. If you *really* wanted to portray Victor to the fullest, then you would have been just as mean to *me* as you were to everyone *else*, and I never *saw* it. You were *always* sweet to me. Your mother just told me not to believe everything I saw and only half of what I heard. I started paying *attention*."

"Terri, I'm *sorry*. I didn't do this to get with you or to hurt you. And I definitely didn't mean to get you . . . well, you know . . . in a motherly way. I had to prove my *innocence*. That's the *only* reason I did what I did."

"No need to apologize, V. I actually understand. Don't know if I could have done what you did, but I understand. I've thought about my situation. I even thought about what *others* would think about my situation. I've discovered some things about life: It is *crazy*, and you only get one life to live! I'll tell you something that might surprise you. I have *thoroughly* enjoyed every minute that you and I have spent. You showed me what it was liked to be truly looked upon and appreciated. *You* are the man I want to be married to. I actually *felt* loved."

"You *are* loved," V said unexpectedly.

"*Am* I? Well, here's *another* shocker, V. So are *you* . . . but then again, I told you *that* when I came in."

V just stared at the beauty that stood before him, speechless. Some tears began to fall down Terri's face, and V got up from his seat and went to her. He grabbed her and held her close while she sobbed in his chest.

"I'm *so* sorry, Terri."

"I *told* you," she said between her tears, "no *need* to be sorry. I'm *good*. If you love me like you *say* you do, then everything is just fine."

"What about Victor? I'm supposed to be getting him out of jail *today*. He'll *probably* want to come home. What do you want me to do?"

"Well, I hope *Victor does* come back home to me. I just hope it's the right one. Be a *man*, V. Do what *you* feel is best for one of three people: the baby, me, or yourself. I'm going to respect whatever you decide, but if you want to continue this love with me, I'll be here for you. If all this sounds strange to you, you're not alone. It's strange to me too. But it's also *my* decision."

She broke from his hold and started to leave the room.

"Terri! What about what the *rest* of the world will say?"

"*Fuck* the rest of the world, V! *Fuck 'em!* Sorry. Damn hormones. I've got to stop cussing for the baby's sake."

With that, she left V with his thoughts. He knew *exactly* what he would do now.

CHAPTER 38

UNCOVERED

"Yes, ma'am . . . Yes, ma'am . . . I didn't know at first . . . He told me . . . Yes, ma'am . . . I'm sorry I didn't tell you, but you figured it out on your own, right . . . ? Yes, ma'am . . . He asked me *not* to, so . . . Yes, ma'am, *you're* right. Again, I'm sorry . . . Sure, *we* can be there. What *time* . . . ? At *one*? Okay, we'll be there . . . Yes, ma'am. See you then. Bye."

"I take it that was Moms, right?" Pat asked Junior.

"Yep. She was *pissed* we didn't tell her about V. But she's cool now. We've been invited to a surprise birthday party on tomorrow."

"Where at? Moms's?"

"Naw. She got permission to have it at Terri and Victor's house. Terri wants me to entertain him while everyone shows up. Hell, might as well call it *V's* house, huh?"

"No *shit*. We're *going*, right?"

"If we *can*. I know it's not my day, but is it okay if I break the news? You know, about us?"

"You *better*, sugar!" Pat smiled.

This time Pat's phone rang.

"Hello . . . *Hey*, Mama . . . ! You're *what*? Flying in this *afternoon*? What *for* . . . ? Just a weekend stay . . . ? Okay, Mama, what time . . . ? Okay, I'll be there to pick you up from the airport . . . Yeah, no problem . . . I'll see you then."

"Junior . . . that was my mama. She's coming in for a weekend visit."

"Yeah, I *heard*. I'm FBI, remember?"

"Ha! You know what, I *forgot* you were FBI."

"*Sure* you did. What time do you have to pick her up?"

"She said the flight comes in at 3:00 p.m."

"Need me to ride along?"

"I'd like *someone* to. She's sort of bossy, and I feel better when someone is with me."

"Okay. Done."

Junior's phone rang.

"*Damn*, we're getting a lot of calls lately. Hello . . . ? Hey, Aunt Jenny . . . ? *Calm* down, what's wrong . . . ? Uncle James had *what* . . . ? A *heart* attack? I'm on my way! Are you guys at the med center . . . ? The heart clinic? Is that new . . . ? Okay, I'll GPS it. I'm on my way and try not to worry. I'm sure he'll be fine."

"Should I have a taxi pick my mama up?" Pat asked. "You have got to go, and I don't know if you'll be back in time."

"Naw. Call V. *He'll* ride with you."

"Okay. I will. You be careful, okay?"

"Yeah, you *too*, baby."

Junior dashed out of the door. Pat picked up her phone.

"Hey, V? This is Pat. I need a favor . . ."

* * *

Judge Campbell had the warden on speakerphone.

"So, Warden, what are these papers that have been laid on my desk?" Judge Campbell asked.

"I don't know what you're talking about, Judge."

"Are you familiar with the TV show *Undercover Honchos*? You *know*, the show where the bosses of companies act like the employees just to see how things are going?"

"Yeah, I've seen it. What does that have to do with *me*?"

"Well, it seems a *lot*. One of the bosses of *your* profession did just that! I have pictures, signed statements, and even recordings of you. All of it tying you in with murdering Judge Mumford. They show the murder weapon in your hand, and it is a clear enough picture of you, Warden! What do you have to say about that? You know this changes everything, right?"

The warden turned pale.

"I *had* to, Bill. I just *had* to. He was getting ready to turn us in with our deal with the colonel. That was just too much money to throw away.

It meant my retirement would be taken care of, and I wouldn't be screwed out of what was mine by the government. I *had* to do it!"

"So you *admit* to killing Mumford?"

"Hell *yeah*! You say you have all that shit on your desk and it's just me and you talking, right?"

"Well, *sort* of," said Judge Campbell.

The New York Police Department Precinct 33 sent a few of their finest to visit the warden. As they entered the warden's office, the judge continued.

"You see, all the evidence I needed to clear an innocent man of a crime he didn't commit, *you* just gave it to me. Yeah, I have some pictures and some recordings, but the recording you *just* gave sealed it. The person in charge of this investigation knew—no, he *felt* that if I told you I had what I *said* I had, that you would *break*. It seems the pressure is too *much* for you, and I have no choice but to have you *arrested* for the murder of Judge Mumford and release Mr. Vincent Taylor from prison. The officers that have arrived will read you your rights."

"*Damn*. Well, I guess I'll have to make *another* major decision."

With that said, he opened his top drawer, took out a pistol, and placed it in his mouth. Before the officers could reach him, he pulled the trigger, and the warden's story was over.

The judge hung up the phone and dialed another number right away.

"Hello, Johnson . . . ? Did the warden just . . . ? That's what I thought . . . Okay, call the cleanup crew and hit me back when you finish over there."

He hung up. "Shit!"

"Did I hear what I *thought* I just heard?" asked the other individual in the room.

"Afraid so. It *appears* that the warden has taken his own life. How did you *know* he would confess?"

"I've been watching him for *months*. He always tried to be the strong one, but I could tell he was weak when he started cutting back on the things he was supposed to do to Vincent Taylor. I *also* noticed that he was not the kind to check up on things before making a decision in his life. But I have a question for you, sir: Why did *you* go along with this plan?"

"I have much more at stake than whatever plans that *he* had. He *never* would have turned himself over if I were honest and told him that the pictures I had of him were ones of him eating at a restaurant and the recordings that I had were not of him anyway. I like Bruno Mars, so those are the recordings I spoke of."

"So, sir, am I able to move into the position right away?"

"You *are*. I have already been given the okay from the Bureau of Wardens. When would you like to start?"

"As soon as that office is cleaned up, sir. Thank you for your assistance in this investigation. I already have my confession on tape, so I'm good. I'll let you get the rest of your papers ready for Mr. Taylor when he arrives."

Judge Campbell stood from his desk and shook hands with Pee Wee. He turned to leave the judge's chambers as **Warden** Pee Wee Bryant!

CHAPTER 39

FINGER LICKIN' GOOD

V pulled into the prison yard, feeling a bit anxious. He didn't like the fact of coming back to this facility, seeing as how he was on death row. Once he got out, he figured he'd *stay* out. But this visit was a bit different from his previous ones. For one, he was going in pretending to be someone else; the next thing was he was going in to get someone out; and finally, he had just had an encounter that confused and enlightened him all at the same time. He thought back to that encounter at the airport earlier that day.

"Okay, baby, you sit tight with your auntie. V's here with me. I'll be okay. See you later."

Junior was still at the hospital with his aunt, and his uncle was stabilized for the moment.

"Do you *see* her?" V asked Pat while at the airport luggage drop off.

"No, not *yet*. Thanks for coming, V. I feel a *lot* better."

"Don't mention it. *Anything* for family."

"Family?"

"Well *yeah*. Junior has adopted you to be with him, so I have accepted you to be one of us. You're *family*, Pat."

"Gee willikers, thanks, Beav!" Pat joked. "No, but *seriously*, thanks. It means a lot to me because *Junior* means so much to me."

"Yeah, I *know*."

"There she *is*! *Mama!* Over *here!*"

Pat and her mother meet up and embrace.

"How was your flight?"

"It was fine. Except for this *one* time. *Turbulence*, child. Thought I was gonna throw up my snacks. Who is *this*, your new boyfriend?"

"No, Mama, this is V . . . er, uh, Victor Taylor. My boyfriend's *best* friend."

"Oh. You're *still* with Junior?"

"Yes. Why do you *ask*?"

"No reason. So Mr. Taylor here is to provide *what*? Emotional stability? Muscles? What, child?"

"No, ma'am, I'm here because this is *my* town, and I know my way around a little better than your daughter, that's all. Now if you have some bags I need to carry, I can do that too," V interjected.

"Okay! Your friend answers *all* your questions?" she said to Pat.

"No, ma'am, but every time *you* ask a question that refers to *me*, I feel obligated to answer. I know more about *me* than anyone else, so if you want to *know* something, *anything* about me, please, Ms. Williams, feel free to ask me," V said.

"Okay! You told him my *last* name, *girl*?"

"I *had* to, Mama."

"Point out your bags and I'll grab them for you," V offered.

Pat's mother did just that, pointing out two big bags and a small duffel bag.

"Okay, let's go," Pat said.

As they were walking out, V overheard a man in the corner in a wi-fi station saying something familiar in a familiar voice.

"Okay, everyone! *Break* the banks!"

V wheeled around and saw a man with his back to him, wearing a thick jacket and had a hat pulled down over his face.

"Colonel?" V inquired. He reeled around to face him. V's mouth dropped. By now, Pat and her mother had turned to see what made V stop.

"Kevin? Is that you?" Pat's mother asked.

"Marian! How *are* you? And is this *Patricia*?" the colonel said.

"Yes, I *am* Patricia. Who are *you*?" Pat asked. "Wait a minute. *You're* the man I bumped into the other day!" Pat said.

"Pat, dear, this *here* is your father."

She looked at him for a minute. He nodded. She ran into his arms, and he held her like a precious jewel. The tears were flowing from them both, and the happiness was inevitable.

"Officer Casey?" V said. "You're the c—?"

Kevin pulled his head up from his hugging. "Can we go somewhere and talk?"

"Sure, but *somebody's* gonna *have* to feed me. Those airline snacks just don't *cut* it!" Pat's mother said.

"I wasn't talking about talking to *you*! I meant *Patricia*," Kevin said. He would take care of everyone's meal, but they *had* to eat at the airport. They found a restaurant that pleased Pat's mother.

"Say, can I have this time alone with my daughter. You guys sit over there, and we'll sit over here. Okay?" Kevin said, or should it be said the colonel?

"What? You can't say what you have to say around *me*?" the mother asked.

"Come on, Ms. Williams. Let's give them their space. It's been a long time," V said.

"Okay," she said, "but I'm not *cheap*," she said to Kevin.

"I got you," Kevin said.

Kevin and Patricia took up residence in a booth across V and Ms. Williams and out of earshot.

"So how's my little girl? Sorry about that. I've been practicing that line for years, and I never realized you would grow up. You're *beautiful* though."

"Thank you. I had *forgotten* what you looked like. Mama didn't keep *any* pictures of you around. You're quite handsome yourself."

"You're *too* kind. So what's been going *on* with you? What do you do for a *living*? Do I have any *grandchildren*? Are you married? Come on, spill!"

"Well, I am *not* married, *no* kids, recently *engaged* . . ."

"Engaged!"

"Shhh, *Mama* doesn't know yet. She will tomorrow though. Don't tell her."

"I won't. Go on."

"Okay. I work for the FBI and was working on a case here in the city. A big case too."

"FBI, huh? Did you catch the bad guy?"

"I wish. If he were sitting right in front of me, I'd handcuff him and drag him in. But I found *you*. By *luck*, I might add. How do you know V . . . Victor?"

"I was about to ask *you* the same thing. I don't know him all that well, but he's helped me with some legal ramifications."

"Did I hear him call you something *else*?"

"No, I don't *think* so. What did *you* hear?"

"I *thought* he said 'colonel.' *That's* the name of the guy who was supposedly the main crime leader of this case we were on."

"Oh. No, I'm pretty sure he said my last name, Casey."

"Are you sure? Well, okay. So what about *you*? What's going on in *your* life?"

"Well, it just so happens that I was about to leave town for a new position."

"Where *to*? It's been *seventeen years* since I've seen you! I don't want to *lose* you as soon as I've *found* you."

"Well, honey, I'm sorry. More than anything I'd like to spend more *time* with you. I've missed you so bad. I would tell you where I'm going, but I signed an non-disclosure agreement and I can't. Not *yet* anyway. Let me get settled, and then I'll call you, okay? Maybe arrange for you to come visit me."

Pat dropped her head. "Really?" Silence. "Okay."

"Don't be sad, Patricia. I *promise* you everything will be better for *anyone* that is associated with *me*. *Okay*, baby?"

"All right. I do have another question: Can I call you *Daddy*?"

A tear formed in Kevin's eye.

"*Sure*, sweetheart. *Anytime.* That's who I *am* and who I've *always* been to you. I've really missed you so much, and it just doesn't seem *fair* that I have to leave. Look, go over there with your mother and send Mr. Taylor over here. I only have a couple of more hours before my flight, but I *have* to talk to *him*."

"Okay. And, Daddy? I just want you to know I *never* stopped thinking about you *or* loving you."

"Me *too*, baby. Me too."

Pat and Kevin embraced before she walked over to V to tell him to make his way over to the table where Kevin was seated.

V came over and sat down.

"So . . . *you're* the colonel? How? And how did you come across *that* name?"

"Why did your mother name you *Victor*? I need you to just *listen*, okay? I'm going to tell you the whole story, but you need to just sit there, don't talk and nod, *got* it?"

V nodded.

"Okay. I'll start with the name. My real name is Kevin Franklin Casey. KFC. Who started KFC? Just thought the name colonel would fit. Get it, Victor? I *can* call you, Victor, right?"

V smiled at the ingenuity and nodded again. He also smiled because his true identity was shadowed, and Kevin didn't have a clue.

Kevin continued.

"A few years ago, I discovered a way to make 'cocaine' . . . I say cocaine, but it's really *no*t. It was made from ingredients that were *not* illegal. Okay, that's how Coke is made in the first place, I know that, but I accidently found a way for my product to be mixed with another compound, and it would result in having the properties of *cardboard*. Once it came in contact with water, within two days, it would return to the powdery substance that could now be used. I had to find a couple of guinea pigs, and you know there are *more* than a number of guys in prison that will go for a high . . . *even* if they don't know what the shit *is*! Now when this combined mixture *was* used, a person would get a high, but it would not endanger their head, heart, or any other bodily function. The person would also be in full . . . I *say* full . . . control of their everyday functions without losing their high. Big Percy knows . . . and I know too because that's the way I would be at work almost daily. Sometimes just to get through the day. I thought to myself, 'You know, you could get *paid* for such a product instead of using it up for *what*? A *high*?' So I approached Mr. Sabino as someone who could make this thing pop off! He turned me down. We're talking multimillions—no, *multibillions*—for *anyone* who would invest in this venture. You'll be glad *you* did. Anyway, Sabino was in that wreck with your father, remember? I really hate to be the one who tells you this, but your father *didn't* die in that wreck. *Sabino* did. I know because *I* was there. When Sabino turned me down, *I* was the one that got drunk and they had to take home. Well . . . they didn't *have* to take me home, but they offered. But *while* I was drinking, I was sharing what my plan *would* have been to your *father*. By the time they got me home, I had started sobering up a bit, and I heard the crash from my house. I got on my ATV and rode down to where the accident was. Sabino was *dead*, and your father was in shock, not knowing *what* to do. I *really* sobered up then and came up with the perfect plan. I convinced your father to fake his death, take over as Sabino. We would bury Sabino in a closed casket, and your father and I would pull off the largest and most *perfect* moneymaking venture *ever*! Before you ask, that's what *makeup* is for. The funeral director was also a part-time movie makeup artist. So we got him to make a mask that resembled the face and gloves that resembled the hands of Sabino and placed them on your father. Sabino lives, Thomas Taylor dies, the venture explodes. So *not* true, as your father is alive and well. So the next step was to gather information of anyone who wanted to purchase this product. By the way, the product is called ghost. These individuals wouldn't have to be on the street making a purchase and then arrested for buying illegal drugs. There would be no *sellers* of ghost, so no one could get *arrested* for possession with the intent to deliver. All these individuals would have to do is send the ghost website $2,000 for the special artistic *gears* that they would receive in the mail. The gears aren't worth *shit*. It's the *box* that means everything. Do you know how many buyers of ghost we were able to get? Now this is *worldwide*, brother—five hundred million! Unbelievable, huh? I *said* worldwide. There are seven billion people in the whole world! Of course, *some* of the buyers had a little more money than others, and they wanted to purchase, say $100,000 worth or more at a time. Some will *use* ghost, some will *sell* it, but no matter the case, they *all* have to pay for it up *front*. Now multiply those *millions* of buyers by *$2,000*! That's at least *$1 trillion*! Man, that's a *shitload* of money! *No one* has *ever* seen the amount of money that *we* will see at one time! If I were to keep it all, I would be the *first* and *only* trillionaire there ever *was*! Wouldn't be able to hide anywhere either. But out of fairness, I had *help*, so I'm paying back. Everyone hasn't even made their order, but enough orders have been made with the shipments gone that we can pop this off now. And *repeat* orders? *Shit*, son! We'll *never*, *ever* worry about money again. The warden was *very* instrumental to all these contacts happening as well as protecting the website, God rest his soul."

"What do you mean 'God rest his soul'? What happened to the warden?" V asked.

"I *asked* you not to talk. He confessed to killing Judge Mumford, and when they came to arrest him, he shot himself through his throat. I know this because I am on top of *everything*. Your brother V thought that I was just a lowly security guard, but think about it: How easy would it be for me to get away with this than, say, Sabino or even you! No one would think that *I* could come up with this or carry it out. Getting into a fight with Cooper, getting put on leave, all part of the master plan! Who would have guessed that *I* was the mastermind behind *all* this? Which makes it the perfect plan, don't you think? Now don't go soft on me and start blabbing to any authorities. *Certainly*, don't tell Patricia! You just *thought* you were wealthy as an acclaimed attorney. As of tomorrow, *no one* that is a part of your life will want for *anything* or feel a sense of need *ever* again. That is, however, *entirely* up to you. I *got* mine. You better get *yours*."

"Can I ask a question?" V asked.

"Sure, I'm finished," Kevin said.

"What did you mean by 'break the banks'?"

"Your *parting* gift at the meeting last Sunday. What *was* it?"

"A piggy bank. Oh shit!" It hit V exactly what it meant. He was to break the piggy bank for further instructions.

"Yep. In that piggy bank lies your fortune. Unless you threw it away. Look, I gotta go. Got more preparations. You understand, right?"

"Yeah, I understand. So I guess I'll never see you again, huh?"

"Probably *not*, Victor. No promises, but the possibility is *very* small. Probably *not*."

"Okay. Well, allow me to say thanks for *all* you've done for me, like the extra *cigs*, helping me with the *phone* call, setting up the meeting with my *brother*, and oh yeah, for helping me out with those six guys that *jumped* me. Thanks for being my friend, Kev."

Kevin looked at who he thought was Victor Taylor with astonishment. He then broke out into a huge smile, got up, shook V's hand.

"No, sir. Thanks for being *mine* . . . *V*," Kevin said.

Kevin walked out of the restaurant, smiling, without his ex-wife or daughter seeing him leave.

V walked back over to the table where Pat and her mother were sitting.

"Where did Daddy go?" Pat said while looking over V's shoulder.

"I'm sorry, Pat. He had to leave. He said to tell you he loved you and told me to tell you he would be in touch shortly. I gave him your info."

"Dammit, what about this *meal*? Who's gonna pay for this *high-ass* airport food?" Pat's mother asked.

"Don't worry. *He* took care of it."

The meal came to $85.

V escorted the two out of the restaurant but stepped back in long enough to place the $500 in the waiter's hand that Kevin placed in V's hand when they shook. He came back out and caught up with them.

"Let's get you girls home, okay?"

CHAPTER 40

THE WEEKEND WARRIORS

"So you brought all the papers for me to sign?" Victor asked V. The brothers finally met up in the same room as before when Victor came to see V.

"I brought them all. Chase Morton prepared them. He *is* pretty good, like you said."

"I *know* my employees."

"Well, aren't you going to read them?"

"Didn't you say that *Chase* prepared these?"

"Yeah, he did."

"Well, hand me a pen, V. I don't *need* to read them. Do you know how much trouble he would be in if he fucked up? Hell, *he* does! Did you stop by the judge's office?"

"*Damn*, Vic, you act like I don't want this as much as *you* do! Yeah! I got *everything*! The main question is, are you ready to get out of this place?"

Victor didn't respond. He was too busy signing papers.

"Vic! Do you hear me?"

"Yeah, V, I hear you, but I'm not listening. You didn't mess up my home did you?"

"Doesn't matter to you. You're not going there tonight."

"What the *fuck*? Are you *kidding* me? That's *my* house, you bastard!"

"Not *tonight*, it isn't! Now you have always called the shots in the past, but *this* one time you will *not*. I will put you up in a hotel for the night. Let me talk to Terri and prepare your homecoming. You *owe* me that."

"Okay, twin. I'll *give* you that. Damn, you *grew* a pair since I've been in here."

"You have *no* idea, son. Now before I release these papers with this evidence about *my* innocence, I need to *know*, how long did you know I didn't kill that man?"

"Hell, son, I've *always* known. With what I have going on in my life, I didn't need your ass around to fuck things up! With *you* gone, I would have it made."

"You know *what*? I ought to beat your ass *again* . . . right now, but I'm gonna play it cool. You're the *worst* brother a person could have, and yet I *still* love you. I just can't *stand* you right now."

"Oh, *boo hoo*. *Cry* me a river, *would* you? *Get* me out of this hellhole and to my hotel room."

"Gladly."

As Victor and Vincent Taylor both walked out of that prison facility, they were both glad to be gone from that place. Victor had *never* experienced anything like *that* before and had a new insight about prisoners. Although he was a defense attorney whose sole purpose was to keep people *out* of jail, now he *felt* for those that had to go. V was relieved as ever knowing that his name would not be attached to the murder of another human being. After learning what he just did about his brother knowing of his innocence, V now knew that he would go through with what he planned to do. He dropped Victor off at the hotel and asked if Marco and Alphonso would do him a favor and watch guard so that Victor would not leave. They said they would for $1 million each, which V gladly agreed upon. For some reason, when he put the numbers together that Kevin had given him, $2 million didn't seem like that much. And with the warden out of the picture, the pot got bigger for everyone. V called Junior and asked if they could meet. Though Junior's uncle was out of danger, so his aunt was okay by herself, she didn't want to leave the hospital. Junior left her to catch up with V. They sat down at a bar where V could get a *real* drink and not a suicide soft drink. V told Junior everything. Junior listened.

The next morning V was awakened by the smell of bacon, eggs, biscuits, cream of wheat, and coffee. There was grape jelly and strawberry jam on the table. He came into the kitchen to find Terri burning. Everything looked and smelled delicious.

"Terri? What are you—"

"It's your *birthday*, dear. This is your birthday breakfast! Happy birthday! You didn't know I could *cook*, did you?"

"To be totally honest with you, *no*, I didn't. *Damn*, it smells good! You didn't *burn* anything either."

"Watch your *mouth*, boy," she said teasingly.

"Man, do I need to go get *back* in the bed so that this can be served in there?"

"Okay, *now* you're pushing it. Ha! I didn't get a chance to talk to you last night. How did *yesterday evening* go?"

"*Yesterday?* Yesterday was a *trip*! He's out, if *that's* what you're asking."

"Oh." A sense of dread gripped Terri. *Now what?* she questioned in her mind. V could see it on her face.

"Terri, you don't have to worry. This may be *my* birthday, but the prizes will *all* go to you. *You'll* see."

V walked over to Terri and pecked her on the lips.

"Thank you for breakfast. Love you," he said.

"You're welcome. Love you too," she responded.

"I'll be right back," V said, leaving the kitchen. He went to the study, closed and locked the door behind him, and grabbed the piggy bank that was on his desk. He took the end of his paper cutter and tapped on the bank until it shattered. Inside was a small plastic bag with paper inside of it. He took out the paper and read the instructions. The instructions took him to a secure website where he was to put the contents on the paper into the required spot. After doing so, he waited for about a minute, and a number appeared on the screen with the account where only he had access. The number read $580,000,000.

"Well, I'll be *damned*! That's over $1 million a person! I just hit the *lottery*! That's right, *me*! Not *Victor*! This is *mine*, and it's a *great* birthday present!"

He closed out of the computer and went to the kitchen to eat his birthday breakfast. *I hope Vic enjoys continental,* he thought.

Later that day . . .

"Does V expect anything, Terri?" Moms asked.

"No. I've got Junior entertaining him until I text him. We got this covered. Just don't forget to call him Victor."

"Right! He's gonna love all this food we're cooking. *All* his favorites too!"

"I know, *right?*"

"Who do we know that rides in a limo?" Moms was looking at the gate monitor.

"What?" Terri asked.

"There's someone at the front gate riding in a limo. That looks like . . . Oh, that's Mr. *Sabino*. Did *you* invite him?"

"No. Maybe *Junior* did. He's *welcome* though."

"Okay, I'll punch him in."

Moms punched a button, the gate opened, and then the limo headed up the long road leading to the house. Eventually, the doorbell rang.

"I'll get it, Moms. Keep *burning*. Ha!"

"That's all I know *how* to do, girl!"

Terri opened the door.

"*Hi*, Mr. Sabino! Glad you could make it. You *are* here for Victor's surprise party, right?"

"Hello, Ms. Taylor. Well, I didn't know anything about no party, but I do have a gift for Victor. Is it all right for me to stay, or do I need to come back another time?"

"No, no, it's fine. Come on in. We're in the kitchen, but if you'd rather watch a movie . . . I mean, TV. The screen is so big it's *like* watching a movie."

"Who is this *we* in the kitchen?" Sabino asked.

"Oh, just me and Moms. You know, the *first* Ms. Taylor. Why?"

"No reason. Didn't want to be surprised *myself*. I'll come in the kitchen, if it's still okay."

"Of *course*. I *offered*, didn't I?"

They entered the kitchen, but Moms didn't notice Sabino.

"Say, Terri, isn't that Patricia at the gate? I like that little car . . . looks like she has someone other than Junior with her."

"Well, she's not going to have *Junior* with her. He's with *Vic*. Go ahead and punch her in. Oh, by the way, Mr. Sabino is joining us in the kitchen. I'll go get the door."

"How are *you* doing, Ms. Taylor?" he asked.

"I'm doing *fine*, and you?"

"I must say it does my heart good to see someone as *lovely* as you in the kitchen."

"Don't you *flirt* with me, Mr. Sabino . . . I might *like* it."

"Ha ha. I'll keep *that* in mind."

Pat and her mother, with Terri, finally made it to the kitchen.

"Hello, Pat! Who do we have *here*?" Moms asked.

"This is my *mother*, Marian Williams. She's here for the weekend, and she had to come along for the ride. Mama, this is Moms Taylor. I never learned her first name."

"Pleased to meet you, Ms. Taylor."

"Elaine. The pleasure's all mine, dear. And you can call me Moms too, dear. It cuts down on confusion of who the *real* Ms. Taylor is of this house." She smiled at Terri.

"Okay, are we all *ready*? I'm going to text Junior for him to start making his way here," Terri said.

"Did you invite *Cassie*?"

"Uh . . . *no*, I forgot, Moms," Terri lied.

"You're lying, but that's okay. *I didn't want her ass here anyway*," Moms whispered.

The front gate had someone trying to gain access. It was the mailman.

"Yes. Hi, Charlie! How can I help you?" Terri spoke to the mailman by intercom.

"Hey, Ms. Taylor. I have a special delivery that I need a signature for. Buzz me *in*?"

"Sure. Bring the rest of my mail too."

"Don't I *always*?"

CHAPTER 41

SURPRISE, SURPRISE, SURPRISE

On the other side of the town, *another* mailman is knocking on Debra's front door. She came and opened it.

"Hello? Did you push my doorbell?"

"Yes, ma'am. A couple of times. I didn't hear anything, so I knocked. I didn't wake you, did I?" the mailman asked.

"No. It's okay. I didn't realize my bell wasn't working. What can I do for you?"

"Oh, I have a certified letter for you that I need a signature for."

"Okay." Debra took the plastic pen attached to the postal scanner and signed in the white box on the machine.

"Hmph. *Fancy!*" Debra said.

"Hey, we gotta keep up with the *other* delivery companies. *Cool,* huh?" he said.

"Yeah. Is that *all?*"

"Yep. The rest of your mail is underneath that letter. Have a nice day!"

"Thanks, *you* too!"

Debra closed the door behind her, went to the kitchen, and sat down at the kitchen table. She opened the certified letter and starting reading.

Dear Debra,

I hope this letter finds you in great spirits and in good health. I've been telling you for months to trust me and that I love you. I know that I love you. I questioned it at times, but that wasn't because of you. That was because of what I was going through. You stuck with me through it all, and I appreciate you for it. Now, if you love me and still trust me like you say you do, there is one more thing you must do. Enclosed in this envelope is a one-way airline ticket. Its destination is where I currently am. Do not pack any clothes, but if you have anything of value to you, such as pictures or documents, pack them. You will not return. Trust me. If you do, every dream you ever dreamed will come true. I will explain everything to you when you get here. If you decide not to come, it will be the worst decision of your life. But I will not beg. I have done what was needed to be done, and now I'm waiting for you. I love you and can't wait to see you.

Kevin

P.S. This will be the last time you hear from me unless you come to me.

Debra looked at the ticket, closed her eyes for a minute, opened them, and then started collecting memorabilia and put it in a duffel bag to accompany her on her trip. She called Uber and waited at the door until they arrived. She loved Kevin, she trusted him, and she was gone.

* * *

"Yeah, I'm heading back to the house now. Bring him *now*. Thanks," V said to Alphonso.

"So you're bringing Victor *home*, huh?" Junior asked.

"Yeah. It's time to get this *over* with. I can't *help* it that it's falling on our *birthday*."

"Have you wished him happy birthday yet?"

"Ha! *That's* funny! Even if I *did*, I guarantee he won't feel too *happy* about it."

"Damn, man! You have been a little bit *too* happy *yourself*. What have you *done*, dude?"

"*You'll* see."

* * *

"SURPRISE!"

V entered the house he had resided in, walked down the hall into the den, and was welcomed with a surprise that almost felled him. He looked at Junior, and Junior winked at him.

"Yeah, *I* was in on this," Junior said.

"Wow! *Thanks*, everyone! I *should* have known," V said.

He hugged everyone that could be hugged and shook hands with those that required so. He found himself full of gratitude that his friends and family would go to so much trouble to give him a special day. Everyone ate, talked, and had a good time . . . that is, until the doorbell rang. V was so caught up in the occasion he didn't pay it any attention. Terri did, however. She froze.

"I'll get it," Moms said. She went to the door only to be greeted by her *other* son draped on his sides by Marco and Alphonso.

"*Vinny?* VINCENT!" Moms squealed as she grabbed her son and hugged him as tight as she could.

"Hey, Moms. What a nice greeting. What's going *on* here? There's a couple of vehicles in the yard," Victor said.

"We threw a surprise party for Victor, but I had no idea *you* would be the *best* surprise of them *all*! Come on *in*! Everyone's in the den."

"I *know* where it is. Come on *in*, boys. Moms, you know Marco and Alphonso, *don't* you?"

"I've *seen* them before. Sorta *rude*, if you ask *me*."

Marco responded, "Yes, ma'am, I can see why you might *think* that, but we apologize if we gave you the wrong impression. We are hired to do jobs, and we're good at what we do. Again, Ms. Taylor, we are sorry."

"Well," Moms said. "All is forgiven. But only if you forgive me."

"For what?" Alphonso asked, smiling. "Nice home."

"Thanks. You can tell the *owners* that in a little bit."

When they entered the room, everyone was laughing at a joke that Sabino had just told, but when they looked up, a hush came over the room.

"Oh *no*. Don't stop on *my* account. Let the festivities *continue*! As a matter of fact, isn't anyone going to wish *me* a happy birthday?" Victor asked.

"Happy *birthday*, Vincent!" everyone offered. Terri was *still* frozen. She didn't know how to react or what to say, seeing as how she had made the decision to choose Vincent over Victor. But *now* Victor was in her presence, and it seemed as if the air was being sucked right out of the room. She *had* to tell him, but she couldn't even look at him. V noticed Terri fidgeting.

"Say, V, let's go talk in the study, okay?" V asked Victor.

"*Sure*. We *need* to talk, my brother. Oh, happy *birthday* . . . uh, *Victor*," Victor said to Vincent.

"You too . . . *V.*"

"Say, you two don't mind if I *join* you, do you? Unless it's a *private* conversation," Sabino said.

"Well, *I* don't think—" Victor said.

"*Sure! You* can come! You don't *mind*, do you, Vinny?" V asked.

"No. No, I guess *not*. It's not *my* house, right?"

"Damn *straight!*" Terri said, finding the nerve to say it as they were walking out. Victor whirled around at Terri, but V grabbed him by his arm and turned him toward the study.

"Will you guys excuse us?" V asked his audience. They reached the study door, entered, and V closed and locked the door behind them.

"Say, before you guys start *in* on each other, I wanted to give you the present I brought for you, Victor," Sabino said to V. As far as he was concerned, the other *brother* was the *other* brother. Sabino reached in his pocket and pulled out a small plastic bag that looked familiar to V.

"Here you *go*," Sabino said, handing it over.

"What's *this?*" V asked, trying not to tip to the fact that he had already seen one similar just that morning.

"The *warden's* cut. *Shot* his fool self . . . *dead*. He can't use it in hell, so I thought I'd give it to the person I felt *deserved* it. Happy *birthday!*"

"What do you mean by giving *my* shit to *this* motherfucker?" Victor blasted.

"Hey, calm *down*, Vincent. You had *nothing* to do with what *we* just pulled off. *Victor* did!" Sabino responded.

"*I am Victor*, asshole!" Victor said.

"What?" Sabino stood back, stunned.

"It's *true. He's* Victor. I'm *Vincent*," V said.

"Well, I'll just be damned!" Sabino said, stunned.

"You shouldn't be *too* surprised. You know *all* about perpetrating someone else, don't you?" V asked Sabino.

"What the *fuck* are you talking about, V? This is Antony Sabino! Who *else* could he be?" Victor asked.

"Why don't *you* tell him who you are . . . *Daddy?* Yeah . . . *I* know," V said looking straight into Sabino's eyes. Sabino looked away.

"*Daddy?* What the hell is he *talking* about, Sabino? Why is he calling you 'Daddy'?" Vic asked.

"Because," Sabino said, while taking off his mask, "that's who I *am*."

Victor and Vincent both looked upon the man that sired them. It was Big Daddy Thomas Taylor . . . in the *flesh*.

"*Hey*, Dad," V said.

"Hello, sons," Thomas said.

"Damn! *Thomas Taylor?* You *knew?*" Vic said to V.

"I found *out*," V said.

V reached out, shook his father's hand, and hugged him. "It's *really* good to see you! I *missed* you. *Bad!* By the way, great *job*, sir!"

"Thanks . . . uh, *Vinny*, right?" Thomas couldn't tell the difference between his boys.

"Yeah, *I'm* Vincent. *He* is Victor."

"Hell, now I'm *really* confused. Why all the *deception?* Oh *wait! You* were in jail, and *your* ass wouldn't help, right?" Thomas said to Victor.

"Well, at least you're smart enough to have figured *that* much out," Victor said.

"*Wow!* My boys. Well, I guess I *did* give the present to the wrong person. *Sorry,* Victor."

"Yeah, *right. Now* what?" Victor asked V.

"Sit down. *Both* of you," Vincent said to his brother and his father. They all sat down, V behind the desk. He noticed another small box on his desk that was addressed to "My very good friend." This was the special delivery that Terri signed for, but V had no idea what was in it. He took the box down and placed it under his desk and then began to explain how things would go.

"Okay. *Daddy?* I'm *glad* that you are not dead. But you now have one of two choices to make: continue being Sabino or leave town for good. But by *no* means will you try to get back with Moms. You blew *that* chance when you decided to go along with the colonel's plans. You will, however, set up an account for her to be taken care of. *Capisce?* And another thing, that place outside of town called Elaine's . . . is that *your* doing?" V asked.

"Yeah. I did it to honor your mother. All the earnings from that place have been banked for her anyway. I was trying to find the right time to present it to her. But as far as your *ultimatums* . . . yeah . . . *capisce.*" Thomas Taylor *did* have other plans about Moms, but he knew his son was on the side of *right*. He hadn't thought this plan out to its finality and didn't consider the consequences. He really had his heart set on trying to be back in her life, but he recognized that couldn't happen.

"Well, you had your chance to be our *father* and *her* husband. She's *happy* now. Does she *miss* you? With all her *heart*, man. But there are just some things you can't go *back* to. Allow *me* to say I'm sorry. Now, as for *you*, Victor, I will let you have this present that 'Mr. Sabino' just gave me. No problem. Even though I know you wouldn't do the same for me. However, I *will* keep what I have *already* received, as well as continue being *you*!"

"*What*? You can't do *that*! You signed a *contract*, remember?" Victor protested.

"Yes, *I* remember. But so did *you*! *Do* you *also* remember signing some papers? Do you remember *reading* any of them?"

"*Huh*? *No*, I didn't feel like I needed . . ." Vic's sentence trailed off into silence.

"A little *too* trusting, don't you think? You didn't think I was *smart* enough to finagle this, did you? No, sir, you will *now* and *forever* be known as <u>Vincent</u> Taylor. Signed over all rights and privileges . . . asshole. You're an attorney . . . Well, you *were* an attorney. If you read what you signed, you'll see that it is legal and binding. No different from the documents you had prepared for me. You'll *also* leave the country. *Everything* has been taken care of. We're even building you a nice little *mansion* on the island where you'll be staying. You'll be in the best hotel until they finish," V instructed.

"What about my *firm*? *You* don't know shit about legal matters *or* how to run a company! How are you going to pull *that* off?" Victor asked.

"That is no longer any *one* of our concerns. The company has been sold. You remember Judge Campbell and his investors wanting to make you a *deal*? You *made* it, brother. Chase Morton will be in charge *now*."

"You *bastard*—$90 million for my *business*?" Victor said, jumping to his feet, heading toward V. Thomas grabbed Victor.

"Sit down, Victor . . . I mean, V. You signed the papers. You fucked up. Live with it . . . and besides, I gave the judge a discount. It was only $65 million," V said.

"*You* . . . Let me go, *dammit*! What about *Terri*? What's going to happen when she finds out that you are not *me*?"

"*Terri*? *Hell*, son, Terri *already* knows! She chooses *me*, boy!" V said. "Oh, before I forget, here," V said while handing him the bag with instructions. "You won't hurt . . . financially, that is. But you do have to go. *My* boys Marco and Alphonso will make sure you get on the flight this evening."

"What do you mean *your* boys? Those are *my* guys!" Thomas Taylor said.

"*Really?* So you're gonna continue being Sabino when you *know* you can't be with Moms anymore? You're going to stay around *now* knowing that *we* know who you *really* are?" V asked.

"No. No, I guess *not*. So how do I get out of here without anyone seeing me? I'm ready to go," Thomas said.

"I've got a secret passage. *Don't* I, Vic?"

Victor was just sitting there, steaming. He was *past* pissed. He would try one more thing before giving in.

"Say, V?" Victor asked. "You say that *Victor* will stay here and *Vincent* has to leave, *right?*"

"That's correct. That's the agreement in the contract."

"So are you willing to put who *Vincent is* on the line? Terri has chosen Victor . . . or *you* at least. But in all fairness, I am *still* the *real* Victor Taylor, and I *deserve* the chance to *remain* Victor Taylor. Now I know that you have *always* been a fair person, so I hope you *will* go along with my proposition."

"*Go* ahead. I'm listening," V said, cocking one eye.

"*Moms* won't lie. Let's stand in front of Moms and ask her to look in our eyes. Let her tell *everyone* here who is *Victor* and who is *Vincent*. Whoever *she* chooses to be Vincent has to leave. What do you *think?*"

"I think you'd be a *damned* fool to take that chance, Vinny."

"*Shut* the hell up, Thomas! This is *not* your battle!" Victor said.

"Yeah, he's *right*, Dad. I don't like it, but he *is* right." V thought about what he would be risking: the life, the wife, the baby, the money. Apprehension gripped him. He really didn't know. Why when he didn't have to?

"*Damn*, you boys are something else! I've *always* been proud of both of you. Victor, good luck. Vincent, like I've always told you, do the right thing . . . *even* if it hurts." Thomas was done. He knew he couldn't raise grown men. They would have to make their *own* decisions. They have *so* far.

V looked down, just thinking. He finally came up and spoke.

"Okay, Victor. I know I may be crazy to even *consider* your proposition, but you know what? I have worked hard to set all this up, to put everything in motion like I have. The more I talk about it, the more I'm about to convince myself to turn you down. But my conscience won't let me. And yes, maybe I should consider that woman in there that is carrying *my* baby and *really* think about what I'm risking. Now I may be *wrong* in the end, but at least I'll know I did the right thing. Know what's *funny*? I know if the shoe was on the other foot, *your* ass wouldn't even go along with this. But I guess that's the difference between you and I, huh, Victor? So, whoever Moms says is Vincent leaves with my boys. No resistance. No defiance. But know something: Terri is *pregnant*, and if *you* remain, that child is to be treated like it really is yours. If you *don't*, contract or *no* contract, you will have to answer to *me*!"

"Terri's *pregnant*?"

"Yes. And the baby belongs to *Victor Taylor. Get* it?" V asked.

"Okay. I guess to the *Victor* go the spoils, right?" Vic said.

"*Clever*, brother. Now *I've* agreed. Do *you*?"

"It was *my* idea, remember?"

"I was *talking* about Terri and the *baby*."

"I guess *I* don't have much of a *choice*, do I? Okay."

"All right then, let's go and get this over with. For *good*."

CHAPTER 42

THE ALL-SEEING EYE

"Hey, where have you guys *been*? You just missed the big *news*! Junior and Patricia are *engaged*! Isn't that *great*?" Moms asked.

"It *is*! Congratulations, guys! I *knew* it was just a matter of time," V said.

"Yeah, me *too*! Where is *Sabino*?" Moms asked.

"Oh, he had another *engagement*. He sends his regards *and* his apologies," V answered.

Victor started in. "Yeah, well, *anyway*, Moms, you know your sons pretty well, *don't* you? You said that the *eyes* are the windows of the soul, right? So if *anyone* knows which one of us is *whoever*, it would be *you*, wouldn't it?" Victor asked.

"Yes, I know you two *pretty* well. Why are you *asking*?" Moms inquired.

Terri stood in the corner of her den, staring at V. At the *moment*, everyone could tell who Victor was "supposed" to be, as well as V, because of the clothes they had on, so Terri knew she was looking at her man. The only thing was her look was a horrified one. She did not like where this was going, and her breathing got shallow. She suddenly felt light-headed.

"Excuse me, Pat. I need to sit down," Terri said, crossing over Pat to get to a seat.

"Just play *along*, okay, Moms? And *Moms*? Don't *lie*, okay?" Victor said.

"Okay. *Why* would I *lie*?" Moms said.

The boys stood side by side while Moms came up and looked both in their eyes. She did this back and forth about three times. She was ready

196

to tell everyone there who was Vincent and who was Victor. Marco and Alphonso stood close by, waiting for Victor's instructions. Patricia and Junior sat by each other, holding hands, although Pat didn't know why Terri grabbed hers. Terri couldn't look. Pat's mother was clueless.

"*This* was a *dumb* game," Moms said.

"I think so *too*," said Pat's mother.

"Why is *that*, Moms?" Junior asked.

"Because everybody here saw Victor hanging with *you* earlier and V being escorted by these *gentlemen*. *Nothing's* changed. They are the *same* as they were when the party started."

Victor stood there stupefied. He could *not* believe that Moms just told the *world*, as far as he was concerned, that *he* was *Vincent* and that his brother was *Victor Taylor.*

V nodded to his new "employees," and they grabbed Victor on both arms and headed toward the front door.

"Gotta go," Alphonso said. "Nice home, Ms. Taylor. Thanks for having us. We'll see ourselves out."

Everyone in the room was silent and wondered what was *really* going on. Victor and his escorts got to the front door when Moms came running up behind them.

"Wait! *Wait!* Where are you taking my son?"

"We're just escorting him out like we escorted him in. He's got a *plane* to catch, and we're just trying to help him not *miss* it," Vido said.

"Well, let me at least say *good-bye.*"

She hugged Victor *tight.*

"*Why*, Moms? You *lied*! You *know* I'm Vic, *don't* you?"

Moms whispered in his ear, tears running down her face, "Yeah, I *know*. I did what was right for Terri and that baby of hers. You would *not* have been good for this situation. Even *you* know that, *don't* you? I tried my *damnedest* to raise you right . . . give you some *standards* about the way you should carry yourself. If you had carried yourself with a little humility . . . just *once*, *none* of us would be in this situation. *You* chose this outcome as much as *I* did."

Victor couldn't answer. He was hurt and didn't care if she saw him cry because that's just what he did—uncontrollably sobbed.

"I am *so* sorry, son, but you'll be okay, *right? Please?* Be okay . . . *okay?*" Moms said.

Victor broke the grip that Moms had on him, turned his back on her, and got into the backseat of the car beside Marco. They drove off, and Moms stared the vehicle off the site with teary eyes. She grabbed some tissue from one of the bathrooms along the way back to the den and tried to compose herself. When she got back into the room, she saw Terri being consoled by V. She was crying on his shoulder. V looked up and mouthed to his mother, "Thank you!"

"You're welcome, baby. You're welcome," she mouthed back.

* * *

Cooper took off this Saturday for a little R & R. He went to his front door to be greeted by the mailman. Certified letter. He had already broken the bank at his household and received the benefits from his investments. He couldn't be happier but knew not to quit his job just *yet*. No more money problems, but he was also instructed not to do anything to bring attention to himself. He couldn't figure out *who* would be sending him a certified letter. He signed for it and took it in to read it.

"Who was that, dear?" his wife called out to him.

"Just the mailman. Nothing important," he responded.

Cooper didn't have to read long. It was only a note, and the note was short. It read,

I told you that you would have a well-whipped ass when I got out. I'm out! Watch your back!

Cooper sat down in his chair and looked around his room.

"*Shit!* I'm not *afraid* your ass! *Whenever* you're ready . . . *I'm* ready!"

He would be rich but not without a price paid back. He would live like this for the rest of his life, even to his death. Cooper jumped at anything and everything. He never did have to fight this fight, but he always anticipated it. What's funny is that Cooper thought this note was sent by V, but actually, it was sent by Kevin. Cooper thought he would hurt Kevin without touching him, but it was Kevin that didn't have to *actually* touch Cooper in order to *touch* Cooper, and he knew it. Cooper never got the chance to truly enjoy his fortune because of fear. He never quit his job because it was the only place he felt safe. *No* amount of money can give one true peace. When someone dies, you *never* see a Wells Fargo truck in the funeral procession.

CHAPTER 43

LOOSE ENDS

Three months later . . .

"That was a very nice wedding gift you gave Pat and Junior. It was *mine* first, but I'm *good* with it. I need to make a fresh start, anyway," Terri said to V.

"Yeah, well, it's *only* a house, right? We're *traveling* anyway. Where do you want to go *first*? Say, how about *Switzerland*? That's where one of my pig sties is."

V was referring to where *some* of his money was. A Swiss bank. When you hear of someone hitting it big, Vincent Taylor hit it BIG. On his birthday, he told Junior that he would give "his" house to him if they got out of this thing alive. This meant that Junior and Pat would have to relocate, but no one knew they would get married so fast. They didn't want to waste another minute *not* being officially married to each other. So they *set* the date for June and *kept* it. Even Pat's mother came around to Junior as far as acceptance was concerned. Moms did the catering, since Sabino, or should we say, Thomas Taylor, gave a substantial gift to her to start her own business. You'd think she would call it "Moms," right? Nope. She called it Big Daddy's Catering Service in honor of her late husband. Thomas was proud, but he didn't reveal who he really was. If he were to teach his sons to do the right thing, he felt he should follow that concept. The city would still know him as Sabino, but he honored his sons' wish and stayed away from Moms.

"So you *said* that once we moved out, you would tell me exactly how *much* money we . . . I mean, *you* have," Terri said to V.

"No, *you're* right. It's *we*. Well, let's *see*. It started off with about $580 mil, then $65 mil on top of that. And then that last box came on my birthday. It was another piggy bank from the colonel with different instructions. Are you *sure* you're ready for this?" V asked.

"Hit me. I'm a big girl."

"Okay. My last transactions totaled over *$7 billion*! Did you *hear* me—*$7 billion! Damn*, I shouldn't have *told* you. You know, the colonel *could* have been a *trillionaire* had he chosen! He was *very* gracious!"

"What? That's *outrageous*! You're *kidding, right?* Is it *real?*"

"It *is*, baby. I *told* you this is going to be all for you, me . . . and the *baby*, of course!"

"Of *course*."

"But trust me, I'm not keeping all my eggs in one basket. I've got accounts all *over* the place. I couldn't *even* have imagined how good things would turn out for us! Thanks, Vic."

"You can say that. *I'll* say thank *you*! Can I tell you something?"

"Sure. Anything."

"I love you."

"Well, I love burgers, and ours is coming to the table now." V was teasing. What he didn't tell Terri was that he took her to the same table in the airport where he last met with his friend 'Col.' Kevin Casey. He paid the waitress $500. He put his finger to his lips to shush the waitress. "Put it in your pocket and keep it to yourself."

He then reached out and touched Terri's hand.

"I love you too, Terri. I really do."

Terri and Vincent planned their adventures and trips, with no reservations or regrets. They could travel nonstop if they chose, or they could buy an island and sit. All was better than good.

Meanwhile, back at the "Taylor" mansion . . .

"Hey, Pat, did I hear the doorbell? I was in the bathroom and thought I heard it," Junior said.

"Yeah, you did. That was the *mailman* dropping off this package."

"Is it for *me?*"

"No, it has *my* name on it."

"Well, *open* it, babe."

Pat opened the box and pulled out a *piggy bank* with a card that read,

Congratulations on your recent wedding! Thought I'd give you a little wedding present. This is not to keep but to break. Hope to see you soon.

Love, Daddy

Pat stood there with her mouth wide-open.

"*Daddy?* The *colonel?* Well, I'll . . . be . . . *damned*," Junior said.

* * *

Victor was lying down, watching satellite TV on a Jamaican island. His house was finished, and it was laid too. He had all the amenities that he felt he needed. He just couldn't live in the USA. He was sipping on a tropical drink he had Dez, his personal valet, make him. When Vic was in the States, he didn't want any hired help. Over here, he demanded it. He was like the king of the island but without the title. Dez catered to his Victor's every whim. Dez didn't have to dress all proper, so he typically wore a "Welcome to Jamaica" T-shirt, khaki shorts, and sandals, and most times he would stay out of sight of Victor . . . until called upon. There was a ringing of a doorbell.

"Yo, *Dez*! Get the *door*, okay?" he yelled out.

Dez went to the door and then returned to where Victor was, escorting a man with Rasta braids and colorful clothing that looked like the Cross Colors brand, with matching shirt and shorts. He was about the same height and build as Victor but just a shade darker skin, with a mustache and a braided goatee. Dez exited.

"*Yo*, mon! Won *qwine?*" the man asked.

"What?" Victor said.

"Oh, so surry boot dat, mon! You don cotch me drift, huh? Tell yuh wot . . . me slow down for yuh. Wot's . . . going . . . on? Won *qwine?*" the man said.

"Oh . . . nothing much . . . I guess. *Who* are *you*, and *why* are you in my *house?* DEZ!" Victor called out.

"Ain't no need to call on Dez, mon. He cool. *Luke* ot me . . . *reel* close. Wha d'yuh see? Or should me say, *who* d'yuh see?"

The man pulled his braids back from his face so that Victor could concentrate on the face alone.

"It's like I'm looking in the mirror! What the *hell*? *Vincent?*"

201

"No, mon. Not Veencint. Me name's Vance. Vancelot Taylor. You tot you were two, no? No, dude. You be *tree*! *I* be de missing piece to de *puzzle*," Vance said, holding up three fingers.

"*Three?* I'm part of *triplets?*"

"*Yah*, mon! I be your *brudda*! So it *must* be in your mind why me 'ere, no?"

"Yeah. Why *are* you here? You *live* here?"

"Yah. Our fahda made sure no one knew boot me, boot me was kept alive for insurance purposes. Me got a little cash, but de old man forget aboot me. Damn. 'Ow mooch did yuh make away wit?"

"What are you talking about?"

"You can play stoopid if you so choose, but me *knows* wot went down."

"I'm not *telling* you *shit!*"

"*Wah?* Why *not?* Boot tree hundred million, *right? Told* you I *knew.* Just tot you might wanted to share."

"Uh . . . okay . . . *yeah*, you're right. What's it to you? How do *you* know about this, anyway?"

"Me knows a *lot* more dan me can tell yuh. Boot me *will* tell you *dis*, mon. You got de fucking *shaft*. Tree hundred million is *chump* change."

"*Chump change?* But I signed *papers*! I *have* what I have because I was *stupid* and careless. What, *you* think you can *help* me or *something*? I'm *not* going to be stupid and careless with *you!*"

"No, mon. Me *knows* me can help. Me see you be *cautious*. Dat be a *good* ting! When *you* be ready, what d'yuh say we go git wot be yours, brudda! Or should me say, wot be *ours*? Wot yuh say to *dat?*"

Victor looked at this stranger who looked exactly like him and his other brother for a minute. He thought long and hard. *Should I trust him? What if he* can *help? Hell, what have I got to lose?*

"Why *should* I trust you? I don't even *know* you. What if you *are* V?" Victor asked.

Vance stood up and started to exit the room.

"*Hell*, mon, you don *'ave* to truss me if you don *won* to. I be *leaving*."

"Wait!" Victor said.

Vance stopped dead in his tracks but didn't turn around.

"What *exactly* do *we* have to *do*? Or what do *I* have to do . . . *Vance*, is it?" Victor asked.

Vance looked over his shoulder.

"So do dat mean you *truss* me now?"

Victor could only nod.

"*Well*, den you 'ave to do wot me *say*. Me promise *not* to steer you wrong and *you* promise to cut me in. Agree to *dat* and you'll *see*, me brudda. You tink you a *king* 'ere? Compare wot you *could* 'ave and wot you 'ave *now*, you ain't got *shit*! But if you give me de power you tink you 'ave, you will tank me later. Victor Taylor's name will be immortalized! *You'll* see!"

Victor looked at his newly introduced brother. He nodded. He smiled. He dreamed.

The end?